ROB COUTEAU is a Brooklyn-born author and visual artist. His publications have been praised in *Evergreen Review*, *Publishers Weekly*, *New Art Examiner*, *Midwest Book Review*, and *Witty Partition*. In 1985 he won the North American Essay Award, sponsored by the American Humanist Association. His work has been cited in books such as *Ghetto Images in Twentieth-Century American Literature* by Tyrone Simpson, *Gabriel Garcia Marquez's 'Love in the Time of Cholera'* by Thomas Fahy, *Conversations with Ray Bradbury* edited by Steven Aggelis, and David Cohen's *Forgotten Millions*, a book about the homeless. His interviews include conversations with Pulitzer Prize-winning author Justin Kaplan, *Last Exit to Brooklyn* novelist Hubert Selby, Simon & Schuster editor Michael Korda, LSD discoverer Albert Hofmann, Picasso's model and muse Sylvette David, sci-fi author Ray Bradbury, film star and bibliophile Neil Pearson, and historian Philip Willan, author *Puppetmasters: The Political Use of Terrorism in Italy*. Couteau has appeared as a guest on Bob Barrett's *The Best of Our Knowledge* (WAMC), Len Osanic's *Black Op Radio*, and on Monocle 24 in Europe. In 2023 he published *Intimate Souvenirs*, a memoir featuring an Introduction by Robert Roper, author of *Nabokov in America: On the Road to Lolita* and *Now the Drum of War: Walt Whitman and His Brothers in the Civil War*. Since 2020 he has devoted himself to republishing annotated texts of important but forgotten authors such as Stanley Marks, Charles Beadle, and Francis Carco.

Spada the Bandit

André Spada

Edited with an Afterword
by Rob Couteau

Originally assembled and edited
by H. Lesley Thomas in 1935

DOMINANTSTAR

ISBN 978-1-963363-03-6

Originally published in 1935 as *Spada the Bandit: The Autobiography of André Spada — Last of the Corsican Bandits* by Grayson & Grayson in Mayfair, London, and assembled and edited by H. Lesley Thomas from material supplied by Spada.

Cover: Spada's mug shot, 2 June 1933.

RobCouteau.com

10 9 8 7 6 5 4 3 2 1

Contents

MITCHELL'S CIGARETTES

SPADA, THE CORSICAN BANDIT

An André Spada trading card, manufactured
by the Imperial Tobacco Company in 1935.

A GALLERY OF 1935

A SERIES OF 50

50

SPADA, THE CORSICAN BANDIT

André Spada, last of the Corsican bandits, was guillotined at Bastia, Corsica, on June 21st, 1935. For eleven years he had terrorized the countryside, and it took a force of 600 men to bring about his capture. For the first twenty-four years of his life Spada was a sober, hard-working citizen, then he suddenly turned bandit and started to prey on his fellows. He soon established an ascendency over the other bandits and became known as " King of the Green Palace" and "Tiger of the Cinarca." Women were fascinated by him, and he is said to have made love as lightly and callously as he took life.

STEPHEN MITCHELL & SON

ISSUED BY THE IMPERIAL TOBACCO CO.
(OF GREAT BRITAIN & IRELAND), LTD.

Reverse side of trading card, which includes the caption: "Women were fascinated by him, and he is said to have made love as lightly and callously as he took life."

SPADA THE BANDIT

To have lived to the full, to have loved, to have fought, to have killed: that is a man's life. And even though the price be death, it would be cheap at that. No man has lived fully till he has loved deeply and often; no man has the right to the title of "Man" till he has fought and won; no man has tasted the fullest measure of power till he has killed.

To regret is weak. I have no regrets, save one; and that is for what happened to Mimi Caviglioli's young brother. Jealousy was the cause, a fierce gnawing jealousy that for a time turned me into a being scarcely sane—an animal. A passion for beautiful women is my only weakness; but it is a weakness that has placed me where I am—behind a grille—and has set the guillotine hungering for my neck. A woman's pretty face accomplished what the Might of France failed to do.

For thirty-three years I existed: for eleven, I have lived. In those eleven years I have crowded more experience, a greater sensation—love, passion, hatred, ambition, yes, and even fear—than a hundred other men in the whole of their lives. I have often been asked, "If you could go back to that day in 1922, the day before the shooting of that sailor, would you have built your life differently? How often and how deeply have you regretted the sudden impulse that drew your gun for the sake of the little flower seller?" But my answer has always been the same: "No, a thousand times no, I have never regretted that impulse that made me an outlaw from society and the 'King of the Maquis.'"

These last eleven years have been so full—full of planning and scheming: planning how to increase my power, scheming how to avoid the forces of the law and those who would betray me if they dared—that I have had but little time for introspection.

Now, since the handcuffs closed about my wrists and I can no longer see the sun rise from behind my beloved Corsican mountains or sink into the misty blue of the Mediterranean, I can look back upon my life as a reader can look back upon a book whose last chapter has been reached and which yet lies open upon his knee.

To me it is a wonderful book. In it is all the glamour and color that can be crowded into so short a space—eleven years. Its pages are written in blood and bespattered with the sweat of toil: but not the toil that most men know, the axe, the plough, the anvil, the bench. My toil has been an unsleeping alertness, as of a wild animal, always on the watch for its hunters, ever ready to pounce upon its prey, never relinquishing its tension lest some false move may betray its whereabouts and the crack of a gun and the searing heat of a bullet shall end its days.

I have no fear when I consider the possibility that before the dawn of another year the guillotine will have claimed another victim and the last chapter of my life will be closed. I have met fear face to face too often to feel it now. Rather I think of Romanetti, of Rutili, of many other true and glorious comrades who have gone beyond and are waiting for me, the last of the banditti, to join them.

So much has been said of our ruthlessness, of our cruelty, of our wanton destruction, that for the sake of my comrades rather than from a desire to whitewash myself, I wish to tell the story of André Spada, the last King of the Maquis—of myself.

When I die the world will rejoice. It will say, "At last the island of Corsica has been freed of that devil who has been sucking its life's blood." But what of the peasants, of the Corsicans themselves? Will they hang out bunting and hold festa when the knife falls upon Spada's neck? Not they! I was born in Corsica. I have lived my life in Corsica, amongst its peasants, in its villages, and I know that on that day there will be barely a dry eye amongst those that are Corsican at heart.

The town dwellers may rejoice, the hotelkeepers, the gendarmes, the city fathers—but not the peasant. I was their protector and their friend, as was Romanetti before me. They knew that so long as they remained true that they had nothing to fear from me. If they were sick or in trouble, if they needed help or money, I was there to provide. The world, they say, is turning to Socialism, to the helping of the poor from the rich man's pocket. If that is so then not only was I King of the Maquis but King of Socialism, for that is how we lived, we bandits, helping the poor at the unwilling rich man's expense.

How long will the hotelkeeper, the smug shop owner rejoice at my downfall? Do they realize how much of their custom, how many of the foreign visitors, came to the island through the glamour of the Maquis? Now that glamour is gone, the reign of the Maquis is ended. Peace and law will now lay their healing hands upon the stricken island. So they say. But when a widowed peasant's only son dies, who will provide for his aged mother? The hotelkeeper, the shopkeeper? Not they! They will be too busy building up their bank accounts. It will be then that the hand of the outlaws will be missed, and the name of André Spada remembered with, maybe, a tear.

Much has been written of the banditti of Corsica, and most of it has been false. How often have the journalists compared us with the gunmen of Chicago? A thousand times if they have once. The Chicago gunmen have spread and thrived on vice: we in a measure have suppressed it. Romanetti, who probably was the greatest leader in the Maquis, was a truly moral and kindly man. I should know; I have served under him as his chief lieutenant and have seen his many acts of kindness and chivalry. True, we have killed, and killed freely; but not wantonly. It has been either in self-defense or to wipe out some great wrong. The Northern mind can scarcely grasp the true significance of our vendettas. To us some wrongs can only be righted by death. It is not a matter of vengeance: it is our honor that is at stake.

The Corsican is a peaceable and quiet man, but do him a wrong that places his honor in danger and he becomes the most implacable of all men. I speak as a Corsican, for I was born and reared in the "Isle of Beauty." My parents were Sardinians, but before my birth they had emigrated to Corsica and settled in the village of Lopigna, where, in 1889, I was born. My real name, by the way, is not Spada but Gavini—André Gavini.

My early days were peaceful and I showed but little of the spirit that one day was to make me the King of the Maquis. Certainly I had my fair share of a normal boy's love of adventure, and even from an early age was greatly attracted to the fairer sex. I suppose I had rather more than my share of conquests in the village, and had to put up with the friendly banter of my friends, particularly of Santu Stephanini, to whom I rather looked up in those days. True, Giovanni Ferrari, with his quick temper and eager gallantry, was one to make their heart beat fast; and Zetto Rutili, later known as the "Lion of Lopigna," was reputed to have had a greater number of fights over girls than any other young man in the village. All the same I seemed to have some fascination that the others lacked that would bring a girl to my hand, as a half-tamed colt to the hand of a born horsebreaker.

Early in life my father set me to work in the forests.[1] The work was hard, and it laid the foundation of my perfect physique without which I could never have withstood the hardships of later life when we had to fight, not only against the police, but against the extreme cold of the Corsican mountains, some of which attain a height of nearly nine thousand feet.

I was not fond of work, particularly under another man's direction. We Corsicans—at heart I am a Corsican, though of

---

[1] Spada's father worked as a charcoal burner and a lumberjack.

Sardinian blood—are an independent and freedom-loving people. It was this aversion to control that later got me into my first real trouble—that and my weakness for women.

It was some years before the War that I became of military age. The idea of service did not appeal to me; besides, there was Maria, I did not want to leave her. I had fought over her with Zetto Rutili and had won. The fight did not spoil my friendship with Rutili. We had loved the same girl; we had fought; I had won. That was all. There was no bad blood about it upon his part; no cockcrowing on mine.

Par bleu, but she was beautiful, was Maria. How could I have joined some regiment and left her? When the time came for me to report for service I failed to do so. They would have taken me, but I sought refuge in the Maquis.

For those who do not know the island I had better explain that by far the greatest part of it is covered by thickly wooded highland—the Maquis. Her population is distributed over the lowlands around the coast. There is no place on earth more ideally fitted as a sanctuary than the Maquis. Dense woods, few roads, crags for lookout posts, caverns to hide in, fresh water in abundance and, lastly, game for the killing, wild pigs and fowls.

There I lived for a while, coming down into the villages, whenever I felt it would be safe to do so, to drink with my comrades and replenish my provisions. And, of course, to drink of another and even more intoxicating wine—the red lips of Maria.

I was perfectly happy in the Maquis. The free and unfettered life suited me. My time I spent exploring and hunting. Fortunately, the various bands of outlaws did not resent my intrusion. The Maquis could hide a thousand men, what difference would one make? Besides, in a way, like them, I was a fugitive from civilization. There was no fear that I would betray them to the police. They left me in peace.

Then came the War. Joining the army in peace was one matter: joining it in war was another. The idea of fighting appealed to me. I suppose, like many another young fool at that time, I was overcome with the glamour of the moment. I came out of hiding and enlisted. Probably I should have been punished for evading military service; but France needed men, young, healthy men who were eager to fight. I was young and healthy and my fighting instincts had been aroused. They enrolled me, and before very long I was drafted to a regiment.

It was not many weeks before disillusionment came. War was not an epic of gallantry, not even to a full-fledged soldier, far less to a recruit: it was a boring grind of dull and, to me, useless and degrading duties. I could not bear the authority, the feeling that I was little better than dirt beneath the feet of my officers and sergeants. At best, I thought, they can but look on me as cannon-fodder. I had always resented authority, and since my recent life in the Maquis this love of freedom had grown beyond bounds. I would not submit to orders. I was probably set down as an ill-tempered and surly cur whose spirit must be broken. I was always in trouble—refusing to obey commands, insolence, indolence. Oh, yes, in their own minds they were probably very much justified: to my mind they were tyrants. After two months I deserted.

II

THE experience gained during my exile in the Maquis now came to my assistance, though avoiding the police in the Maquis was a childlike pastime compared with avoiding the military authorities in France. As I have already said, the Maquis is the most perfect refuge on earth—to a Corsican; I would not describe France in wartime as being such. However, eventually I wormed my way to Marseilles. The Maquis was my objective: once let me reach Corsica and I would be safe from recapture. Marseilles seemed to me to be the best jumping-off point for the island. Perhaps I was unwise in my choice. I do not know.

I reached the city in the dusk of an autumn evening and at once made my way towards the docks. Here I encountered my greatest difficulties. Even in the outlying districts it had been hard to avoid capture. Walking into Marseilles was like putting one's head on a railway line and hoping the train would not run over it, for the docks seemed lousy—there is no other word for it—with the military. However, I had to take the risk, for there are only three ways of reaching Corsica—swimming, flying, or by ship. As the first two were obviously impossible, there alone remained the ship, and ships sail from docks and harbors. It is a pity that the same idea occurs to those in authority and that they plaster the quays with soldiers and police to see that no unauthorized person enters or leaves the port. However, it is the way of the world.

I had hoped in the darkness to fall in with some friendly seaman who would give me the information I desired—the whereabouts and movements of some vessel destined for Corsica. I had no luck and was reconnoitering on my own in the hope of recognizing some island craft when I was challenged by a suspicious sentry.

"I am a seaman," I told him, "looking for my ship."

"And your ship's name?"

I thought quickly.

"The Marie Blanche of Rouen."

The man looked keenly at me.

"The Marie Blanche of Rouen? There is no ship of that name in port, my friend. I must ask you to come and see M. le Commandant."

The game was up, I could see that. There was nothing for it but to fight my way out. I took a lightning blow at the man's stomach, hoping to wind him. My aim was not quite perfect, for although he dropped his rifle and doubled up, he had sufficient breath left in his lungs to let out a fearsome bellow. At once in the darkness I heard a clatter of running feet on the cobbles. Diving down an alleyway, I tried to dodge my pursuers, but they were sufficiently close behind me to make my task difficult.

After a stiff chase I came upon a lighted quarter of the town and, since a running man would have aroused suspicion, I slackened my pace and strolled up the street and along the next trying to look unconcerned. I felt moderately safe for the moment, as my pursuers had caught sight of little more than a shadow as I made off, and I did not suppose that my friend the sentry would as yet be sufficiently recovered to join in the hunt. However, it would not be long before my description was circulated, and then I would have my work cut out to evade capture.

A voice at my elbow made me jump.

"*Pourquoi promenez-vous?*"

A woman of the street. A woman, did I say? A girl. She could have been no more than eighteen or nineteen, a slight young figure in a blue coat and skirt, a scarlet hat and high-heeled slippers. She had hair, black as a storm cloud, that was cut in a straight fringe across her brow and jutted out in two sickles from beneath her hat on either side. Her face was white and her lips vied with the scarlet of her hat.

"*Pourquoi promenez-vous?*"

The password of the woman of the street. If I could get this girl to take me to her room I would be safe, at least for the moment.

"I am a soldier on furlough, Mademoiselle. I look for enjoyment—and company."

She smiled the set, mirthless smile of her profession. A smile that curls the lips but brings no light to the eyes.

"I can give you both, monsieur. And I know of a little restaurant where the wine is good. We can have supper."

"Your name, *chérie*?"

"Simone. And yours?"

"André."

Thus we were introduced, and Simone led the way to her little restaurant where the wine was good and we could have supper.

Ah, but she was sweet, was little Simone, as yet unspoiled by her profession. I asked her why she had entered it.

"*Mais, pourquoi non, mon André*? One must live, so why not by love?"

We supped, we talked, we laughed, we drank, and so entertaining a companion I found Simone that I almost forgot the military police who were no doubt scouring the town for me. But I have always been like that. Give me a pretty woman whom I can love, even though it be but for a very little while, and I can forget the danger that may be threatening me. True, Simone was what she was, and one is not expected to fall in love with a woman of her class, nevertheless I found myself coming under her spell even as she was coming under mine.

The laughter that came from her painted lips now reached to her big brown eyes, and there was a flush on her white cheeks that the wine had not brought to them.

How she guessed I cannot tell, but a woman often knows one's secrets without a word having passed. It was in her room later that night she said:

"André, you are a deserter from the army, *n'est-ce pas*? Why, for you are no coward?"

It was no good bluffing. If I had lied to her she might have called in an *agent*. I told her everything as she sat on the edge of her bed, swinging a long, silk-clad leg with a little red shoe dangling precariously from her toes so that I watched her, fascinated, as I spoke, expecting to see that little shoe fly off and hit the wall. I told her of my love of freedom and my hatred of authority. When I had finished she nodded her head several times and slipping off the bed, came and sat upon my knee, one slim arm about my neck.

"I know, *mon brave*. My parents, they would have put me into the laundry, and there I would have had to work, day in, day out; each day like the other, no new faces, no new excitements—dull as hell, André, and that old hag standing over us with her horrible, toothless face, crying, 'Now, Simone, my girl, we don't pay you good money to chatter!' Here I am free, I can choose my own friends, live my own life."

For three days I remained there, hidden by Simone while she kept watch on the docks in the hope of finding a ship to carry me across to the island.

She would take no money from me except for the food she bought in the little restaurant below. I begged her to, but she set her lips in a scarlet streak across her face and resolutely shook her head.

"From the others, yes. From you, André, no. I told you I took to this life because of love. I lied—lied to myself as well as to you. The other—it is not love. I did not know what love was, André, till you came here."

There were other girls in the same house, six or seven I should say. Some young and comparatively unspoiled, as was Simone, others older with the lines deeper about their mouths, their eyes hard. There was one, Marie. She was small and cheeky, young, no older than Simone. Sometimes I would meet her on the stairs or in the restaurant, that always smelled of garlic, and she would give me a sidelong look and curve her lips in a provoking way. She was a little devil, was that one. On the evening of the third day I had been there I met Marie on the stairs and, as usual, she looked at me in that way, curling her lips and glancing up at me through her lashes. That time it was too much for my hot blood, and I caught her roughly to me and kissed the silly smirk from her lips.

Presently I saw that she was looking at something over my shoulder with a queer light in her eyes. Abruptly I swung round to follow her gaze, but the well of the staircase was empty and dark, only I heard a light step on the stairs as though of a woman running, and then the door into the restaurant slammed. I swung back to Marie.

"What was it, you little devil?" I demanded. "What were you staring at?"

She smiled back at me, an odd, mocking smile.

"N'importe," she answered softly. "Ce n'était pas rien." And she was gone.

I went back to Simone's room. A quarter of an hour later the door opened and Simone entered.

"Voilà, M. le Capitaine! There is André Gavini — the deserter."

As I passed out between an escort, I looked at Simone. She was seated upon the edge of her bed, swinging one long, silk-clad leg, her little red slipper dangling from her toe. With a tiny clatter the slipper fell at my feet, and as I stooped to pick it up something warm and moist fell on to the back of my hand. A tear?

At the court martial I was sentenced to three years imprisonment for desertion in time of war.

III

The War was over. Once again I was returned to my beloved Corsica and had settled at my parents' house in Lopigna. As one must work to live, even in Corsica, unless one is a rich man or a bandit, I went back to my old occupation, that of a forester.

There were still many of my old friends at Lopigna, though some had fallen in the War, and Santu Stephanini, one of my greatest comrades, was serving a stretch of five years at Fresne Prison.

Soon I had resumed my carefree life, dancing at the cafés and inns, and drinking nightly with such good comrades as Zetto Rutili and Giovanni Ferrari. There was also Giocundi, the woodcutter, but I had little use for him—a sly, sneaking fellow: the sort you would expect to stab you in the back. Marie was married, but I was free of that old passion: there were many other lovely girls in Ajaccio and Lopigna. There was one, Zizi Nicollette, a little flower seller, who was as pretty as the flowers she sold, with her dark eyes and her red cheeks. But none of us made love to her or teased her as we did the other girls. Zizi had fallen when she was a child and was a cripple.

I can see her now, if I close my eyes, as she walked between the tables. She was like a pansy that has been broken by the wind: too tender a bloom to pluck. Few of us could deny her a coin; we were always well rewarded by the way her dark eyes would sparkle and her face would flush with pleasure.

One day Zetto Rutili came to me in great excitement.

"Have you heard the news, André?"

"News, *mon ami*? There is no news in Lopigna these dull days."

Rutili laughed gleefully.

"It is Santu Stephanini, he has been released from Fresne Gaol and has returned."

That was news indeed.

"*C'est bon*, tonight we shall celebrate, Stephanini, you, I, and Ferrari. It is a fête day in Lopigna. Let us meet at the Café Marguerite."

That night Lopigna was in festal mood. The houses had been decorated with flags and every light in the village seemed to be blazing out on to the streets. The cafés and inns were crowded out. People had come in from the surrounding villages, even from Ajaccio. Sailors on leave from their ships, determined to make a night of it. Everyone was dancing, and if they were not dancing they were drinking. Most of them were doing both. A drink with a girl upon your knee, she sipping out of your glass; then a dance; then another drink with, maybe, another girl.

We four, Stephanini, Rutili, Ferrari and myself, were not yet troubling with the girls. We were content to be alone, renewing our old companionship, now that Stephanini had returned. We drank, of course, freely; that and the general excitement and the thrill of having Stephanini back with us may have accounted partly for what took place.

Zizi Nicollette was there, naturally, her basket of flowers on her arm and a happy smile on her lips.

"Oh, André, if I could only dance!" she cried as she passed our table. "Isn't it all so exciting—the people, the lights, the dancing, the music? And have you seen the Italian sailors? Marianne tells me that they are from the *Principe di Savoia* in Ajaccio Harbor!"'

"Keep away from the Italian sailors, *ma petite*," I warned her. "You are far too pretty tonight."

She flushed, and her dark eyes danced.

"Oh, André! Me, pretty!" And she went off laughing.

Presently a group of the Italian sailors came in and settled at a table in the corner of the café. They were all laughing and singing very loudly, and it was easy enough to see that they were far gone in drink. As the evening wore on, the noise and excitement increased. The café girls were shrieking and the men shouting so loudly that one could hardly hear the music.

Then in a corner I saw little Zizi Nicollette in the arms of one of the drunken Italian sailors. She was beating at his face and chest with her bony little hands and crying. Her pretty face was screwed up into an expression of fear and disgust. It was perfectly plain to see what the fellow was up to. There was a door at the back of the café: he was trying to edge his way out through it with Zizi in his arms. If she had been one of the common café girls I would have said nothing. But it was Zizi, about the only girl I had ever really reverenced.

We are a hot-blooded race, we Corsicans, and almost before I realized what I was about I had snatched my gun out and shot from beneath the table.[2]

One moment the café had been a bubbling cauldron of noise: the next—silence.

The Italian let go of Zizi and slowly spun round. The crash of his fall rattled the glasses on the tables.

For an instant we were as quiet and still as a waxwork show, then the voice of the proprietor rang out.

"No one is to leave the café. You, Jean, run for the police."

I had slipped my gun back into my pocket and was sitting—as the others—waiting. No one dared leave the café for fear of being suspect. After that first silence everybody started talking again, but in a hushed sort of way. One or two of the café girls showed signs of going into hysterics and had to be silenced by Madame. An Italian sailor was being noisily sick in a corner.

I felt safe enough, for only my three companions could possibly know who had shot, and they, I knew, would sooner die than give me away. I think that the virtue of honor is more highly

---

[2] The man who attacked the sailor, Jean-Dominique Rubrini, surrendered to authorities a few days later. It isn't clear why Spada continued to take credit for the assault.

developed in the Corsican than in any other race. To us it is an unwritten law that the Corsican shall never betray his companions. Many a man has gone to the guillotine rather than break faith with his code.

It seemed an eternity, though it could not have been more than a few minutes, before Jean, the potboy, arrived with a *brigadier* and three gendarmes.

The gendarmes at once mounted guard over the door and the *brigadier* began his inquiry.

First he made certain that the sailor was dead. There was little doubt of that. When I shoot to kill—I kill.

"Who is this man?" he demanded.

One of the sailors stepped forward and let loose a flood of Italian. The *brigadier* raised his hand.

"*Dîtes en français!*" he commanded.

In fiendishly bad French the man told him:

"It is Luigi Gonzaletti, of the ship *Principe di Savoia*, now lying in Ajaccio Harbor."

The *brigadier* wrote.

"And who shot him?"

No one answered.

"Surely someone must have seen the shot fired?" he shouted angrily. "No one leaves this café until I know the truth."

It was then that a girl stepped forward, one of the café girls, a spiteful vixen of a creature with slant eyes, a tousled mop of hair and a weak, sneering mouth.

"Well?" barked the *brigadier*.

The girl looked across at our table.

"*C'etait lui,*" she said.

"*Comment?*"

"*Lui.*" She pointed straight at Ferrari, who was sitting on my right.

"It is a lie!" I cried, jumping to my feet. "The girl is crazy. It was—"

Ferrari dragged me down on to my chair again.

"Be quiet, you fool," he whispered. "Let them take me. They have no evidence. My gun is clean, while yours ..."

I would have given almost anything to have put a bullet into the gendarme who advanced and snapped the handcuffs on to Ferrari, but it would have done no good.

They led Ferrari away,[3] jostling a passage through the crowd. As soon as they had gone, I took Stephanini and Rutili to a quiet place where we could talk the matter over. News of the killing had soon spread, and as we forced a way through the crowded streets we heard on all sides:

"... at the Café Marguerite ..."

"What happened?"

"... an Italian sailor ... off the *Principe di Savoia* ..."

"Yes, dead; quite dead."

"... Giovanni Ferrari ..."

"I can't let them hold him," I said; "I've got to go and tell them the truth."

"Don't be such a fool!" urged Stephanini. "What can they do to him? They will soon learn their mistake. No one can ever find out who shot the sailor."

Reluctantly I agreed, but it ate into my conscience to know that Ferrari, my friend, was lying at the police house in Lopigna, accused of a crime that I had committed.

---

[3] In most accounts it was Rutili who was falsely accused and arrested, not Ferrari.

IV

All that night I paced up and down my room. I could not rest for thinking of what might happen to my brave comrade, Ferrari, who had been willing to place himself in danger for my sake. The more I thought of it the more convinced I became that I was playing a coward's part. The advice of Stephanini and Rutili might be prudent, but I am not a man to hide behind another's back when there is danger about.

Twice I got as far as the street determined to present myself at the house of the *agent de police* and tell him that it was I, not Ferrari, who had shot the Italian sailor, but each time I went back to my room and resumed my pacing. What good would it do? I argued. They would probably hold us both, and not only would I have failed to save Ferrari, but I would have placed my own neck in the noose, or, rather, on the block.

It was towards dawn that the solution came to me.

I would go to Romanetti, the "King of the Maquis," and ask his help. We Corsicans all knew how often Romanetti had helped when a man was in trouble, and had learnt to rely upon him. Why should he not help me?

The sky was lightening above the mountains as I stepped out into the street, and, when I entered the Maquis, the first sleepy notes of a waking bird came to my ears. Soon the woods were ringing with their song and chatter. As I reached the clearing, where I knew that I should find the hut of Giocundi, the woodman, the first rays of the sun came slanting down through the trees.

Giocundi was still asleep, but came to the door, rubbing his eyes, his face looking even more pinched and mean than it did in the light of full day.

"What do you want?" he growled.

I told him.

"You want to find Romanetti? How should I know where he is?"

It was well known amongst us that Giocundi was one of Romanetti's spies. I did not tell him this, but, instead, I mentioned the possibility of a reward for the man who would lead me to Romanetti.

Putting his head on one side he squinted at me while he rubbed the bristles on his chin with his horny thumb. At last, as though satisfied, he jerked his head.

"Very well. Come inside. At least we can have breakfast first."

I shall never forget that journey to the mountain lair of the King of the Maquis. We climbed up and up, at times traversing what were practically goat tracks with a drop of many hundreds of feet upon one hand, and upon the other, the cliff soaring up above us.

Several times we were challenged by Romanetti's outposts, but, after a brief explanation from Giocundi, were allowed to proceed.

Finally, after several hours hard going, we came upon Romanetti's headquarters, a group of strongly built stone huts with a surrounding wall and a fosse set about them. The site had been well chosen from a strategical point of view and, to me, appeared practically invulnerable.

There was a further parley with the pickets at the entrance, but at last I found myself standing face to face with Nonce Romanetti, the greatest outlaw in the whole of Corsica.

I do not know, but I seem to remember a sensation of disappointment at sight of him. One expects, I suppose, that a brigand chief shall look the part. In a way Romanetti did. He was splendidly clothed in a velvet suit with bell-bottomed trousers. There was a knife in his sash and a huge sheepskin rug over his shoulder, for the mountain air is very cold.

On his head was a scarlet woolen cap. *Ma fé!* he looked a king, but his face was too kindly for that of an outlaw. His beard was neatly trimmed, his moustache was combed, his eyes beneath his broad forehead looked out almost dreamily upon me. Yes, Romanetti had the face rather of a philosopher than of a bandit.

"What can I do for you, young man?"

His voice was deep and kindly.

I told him. And as I spoke he watched my face keenly. At length he nodded.

"*Hein?* You killed the sailor because he would have ravaged the little flower seller. You did well, my friend, though death was too good for such a one."

"And you will help me? You will send to the police and obtain Ferrari's release in exchange for me?"

Romanetti stroked his beard, contemplating me with his big, soft eyes.

"You should have been one of us, André Spada. You do not lack courage or loyalty. Yes, I will help you. Giocundi!"

The woodman came running.

"Go to the *agent de police* in Lopigna and tell him that André Spada is with me and confesses to the killing of that sailor. In return for Ferrari's release I shall see that Spada surrenders to him. Understand? Bring back the reply to me."

When Giocundi had gone Romanetti turned to me.

"Until we receive their reply you must not leave the camp, Spada. I have made myself responsible for your surrender, should they release Ferrari."

That was my first personal contact with Romanetti's strict code of honor. The police were his enemies, but if he gave his word that I would be delivered to them in the event of Ferrari's release, delivered I would be, even though it were my dead body slung over a horse's back.

The police, however, did not put the same trust in Romanetti's honor as did the peasants of Corsica. Perhaps they suspected a trick. At all events the following day Giocundi returned with the insolent reply that "a bird in the hand was worth two in the Maquis."

Romanetti seemed unmoved by this lack of trust. Dismissing Giocundi, he turned to me.

"I am sorry, Spada. I did what I could for your friend. The police have refused my offer. You are now free to go."

I found my way back to Lopigna determined to do what I could for Ferrari.

My first action was to call a meeting with Stephanini and Rutili at a café. They listened dubiously to what I had to suggest.

"I do not like it," growled Rutili. "Stephanini and I are to go before the *agent de police* and swear that it was you who killed the sailor. What chance have you then of escaping the guillotine? They have only that girl's word against Ferrari. No, my friend, it is madness."

I argued. I pleaded.

"But see, Rutili. Am I the sort of man to let a friend suffer for what I have done? They may not execute Ferrari; they will at least condemn him to a long term of imprisonment at Ajaccio Gaol."

At last I managed to get them to agree, and it was with an odd mixture of fear and hope that I waited to hear about their interview with the *agent*.

As soon as I caught sight of them returning I knew that they had failed.

"That *agent* is a pig and a son of a pig," was Stephanini's first comment. "We swore that it was you who shot the sailor and that if he liked we could bring other witnesses—though who else we could have found to swear I do not know—but he said that if the whole of Lopigna should come and testify on his doorstep he would not release Ferrari. He talked about our trying to 'impede the course of justice,' and warned us to be careful."

"Yes," cut in Rutili, "he says that he is certain that Ferrari is the guilty one and that we are only trying to throw dust in his eyes. He says that he is determined that Ferrari shall not escape the guillotine. Tomorrow he is to be taken to Ajaccio prison to await his trial."

That set me thinking, and before nightfall I had completed my plans. That night I slept peacefully, certain that on the day following Ferrari would be free.

I kept watch on the *Poste de Police* until I saw Ferrari set out for Ajaccio between two gendarmes, Caillard and Antoine. Few knew the country better than I did, and already I had decided upon the spot where I should intercept them.

By taking a shortcut through the Maquis I arrived long before Ferrari and the gendarmes at a point where the road dwindled to a mere track that wound its way about the hill. I chose a spot where a big rock screened me from the gendarmes' approach and waited.

Before me the ground fell sharply away to the valley in a cascade of boulders. In the distance I could see the vivid blue of the Mediterranean winking in the sun. It was very peaceful there and hot, the sun striking back from the rocks. Somewhere close a bird was singing. It was difficult to believe that in another few minutes, if the gendarmes did not listen to reason, death would be let loose on that quiet hillside. I had to look down at my two guns, gleaming in my waistband, to realize it was true.

The clink of a shoe against a stone brought me to the alert. Ferrari and his escort were approaching. As they reached the rock behind which I sat I stood up and blocked the path.

"Stop!" I cried.

The right hands of the gendarmes dropped to their guns, and the taller, Caillard, demanded:

"Well, *mon brave*, what do you want?"

"You know well enough," I told him. "It was I, Spada, who shot that Italian. Take me to Ajaccio and let Ferrari go."

Caillard only grinned.

"So? I have heard that story before, my friend. Now stand out of the way like a good fellow and let us pass."

"I will not. I tell you—"

"Stand aside!"

"He is innocent. Let me—"

"Stand aside, I say!"

I am as quick on the draw as any of your Chicago gunmen. My two guns barked as one.

Antoine slumped and fell where he stood. Caillard threw his arms in the air, spun about and toppled over the edge. His body went bump—bump—bump down the boulders till finally it came to rest, sprawled out some hundreds of feet below.

Antoine lay very still—on his face—his fingers crooked as though he had been scrabbling in the dust. The whole front of his forehead had caved in by the force of my bullet at so close a range. With my foot I rolled him over the side to join his comrade below. He, too, went bounding and bumping down the hillside.

Then all was silent again. The bird had stopped singing, but the sun still beat up hotly from the rocks. Below in the valley a woman was hanging out a white sheet to dry. I could see it flapping slowly in the breeze.

"And now what?" said Ferrari.

With a jerk I turned round to face him. I had just killed two men, but oddly enough I felt quite calm. Drawing out a packet of cigarettes, I tossed one to Ferrari and lit another for myself.

"I suppose you realize," I asked him, "that we are now outlaws?"

Ferrari nodded.

"The police will never rest until they have sent us to the guillotine."

I sat down on a boulder and puffed slowly at my cigarette. It was like a dream, sitting there and smoking calmly when only a few minutes earlier I had killed two gendarmes. I felt no more excitement than I would if I had killed a couple of chickens for dinner. From now onwards we were marked men. It would never be safe for us to appear in any of the villages or towns. It would not be long before the police at Ajaccio would begin to grow uneasy at the non-arrival of Ferrari. A search party would be sent out and the dead gendarmes would be found. It was for this reason I had rolled Antoine over the edge to join Caillard, with the hope that it might give us an hour or so extra start.

At length I turned to Ferrari.

"You had better join one of the bands of outlaws," I advised. ' You will be safe then. I should ask Romanetti if he will enroll you. His is the most powerful band, and he is the best leader and a very fine man."

I told Ferrari briefly of my visit to Romanetti's mountain camp.

"And you, my friend?"

"*Moi?* Oh, for the moment I shall be all right. They will not know at once that it was I who killed the gendarmes. Tonight I shall go to my cousin, Stephano Madasca. Tomorrow morning early I shall leave the island."

So it was agreed, and as it was not safe to remain where we were, Ferrari set off up the hillside to the Maquis in search of Romanetti and I made my way towards Madasca's house.

It was late afternoon and Madasca was milking his goats when I arrived. I knew that I could trust Madasca so I told him everything. As I spoke he sucked in his breath and his eyes sparkled.

"*Bon Dieu!*" he cried, when I had finished.

"You are the very devil of a lad, André. Yes, you can hide here tonight. There is hay in the loft, you had better sleep there. Tonight I shall arrange with a friend who will take you off tomorrow morning in his boat. He will want paying well. You have money?"

I told him that I had and so it was arranged. That night I made a bed for myself of hay in Madasca's loft and settled down to sleep with a clear conscience as if I had worked the whole day in the woods.

I seemed hardly to have fallen asleep when I was sharply woken up by Madasca shaking me by the shoulder.

"Psst!" he whispered in my ear. "The devil must be on their side. The house is surrounded by the police. We shall have to try and shoot our way out."

"We?"

"Yes, you fool! Do you think that I shall stand aside and see my mother's sister's son shot down like a bolted rat?"

In the loft it was dark, but as I peered out into the yard I could distinguish objects in the half-light. Something moved in the shadows and my hand dropped to my gun. But it was only one of Madasca's goats. It came out into the yard, looked about and bleated nervously.

I felt Madasca's grip on my arm tighten.

"There!" he breathed. "In those shadows beyond the sty."

I looked and, sure enough, there was the *kepi* of a gendarme. As my eyes grew accustomed to the half-light I made out another, and another, and then a fourth moving beneath the mulberry tree by the gate.

"And at the back, too," whispered Madasca. "*Regardez*, through this window."

I looked and saw more *kepis* and what I took to be rifle muzzles sticking up from behind the bushes, near where the River Cravone skirted Madasca's ground.

Madasca, who had gone to guard the front window, once more appeared at my elbow.

"If we can break through them make for the beach, André. I have arranged with Marchi to take you across to France. He will have a fast motorboat waiting."

A shot rang out and my muscles tensed expectantly. Action was better than this waiting in the dark.

There was a sound of footsteps in the yard below. A *brigadier* of police had stepped out from behind the goat shed and was looking up at the house.

"*Holà*, Spada! Come down before we smoke you out like a rat."

I took a snap shot at him over Madasca's shoulder and had the pleasure of seeing him drop his gun and bob out of sight holding his shoulder.

"*Fripons!*"[4] I yelled. "Come and get me if you can."

For a moment there was silence; then came a spatter of bullets; some flattened out on the walls, a few ricocheted off and pinged away into the darkness, several others smashed through the windows, causing us to duck quickly amid a shower of glass.

I heard Madasca chuckle grimly as he snuggled the butt of an ancient shotgun into his shoulder and started peppering the police. His chuckles turned to curses when an inhuman shriek from the yard told us that a stray bullet had caught one of his beloved goats.

There was sufficient light for us to hold our own, for the police dare not come close enough to the house to fire it—they presented far too good a target for us—and we had little to fear from their rifles, for we were well protected by the thick stone walls.

Presently there was a bustle amongst the attackers. They were advancing—but each man had a large steel shield before him against which our bullets were useless. It was clear enough that we were done for. In a few minutes the cottage would be a

---

[4] Rascal.

bonfire and we would either be roasted alive or forced to come out, as the *brigadier* had said, like bolted rats.

They were pulling down Madasca's rick, tying the hay and straw in bundles and tossing it to the foot of the house. Billets from the woodpile were added. Soon they would strike a light.

Then as we waited there came the sound of firing from a little distance. The police paused in their work, and those in the yard retreated to the shelter of the goat shed as though uncertain.

Presently there came the cry *"C'est les bandits!"* and a general scattering of the police.

It was Romanetti and his band. One of his spies had warned him of the police's intention to raid Madasca's house, and he had come only just in time to save us.

I tried to thank him, but he waved it aside.

"It is nothing, my friend. Perhaps one day you will do the same for me. Who knows?"

He asked me if I intended to join him, but, foolishly perhaps, I refused. I told him that it had been arranged that Marchi was to take us across to France.

Romanetti laughed a little scornfully.

"You will not stay long there, my young friend. You are far too good a son of Corsica. You will see. The Maquis will call you and you will return. When you do, remember that Romanetti is your friend."

With that he was gone, and he was barely out of sight before I regretted my decision. Still I had said I would go, and go I would.

We knew that we had nothing further to fear from the police that night, even though Romanetti had returned to his camp. It was enough for them that the "King of the Maquis" was in that district for them to give it a very wide berth.

The dawn was just breaking when Madasca and I came out upon the beach and saw Marchi and his boat waiting for us.

V

My objective was Spain, Barcelona for preference, for I knew that city but had never come under the eye of the police there. Spain, however, was far too long a distance to attempt in Marchi's boat, so it was agreed that he was to land us as near to Marseilles as was safe. From Marseilles I could work my passage to Barcelona. My main concern, in any event, was to get off French territory as quickly as I could.

The sea was like a sheet of glass and the sun was hot on the boards, so I found a shaded corner under a tarpaulin and dozed for the greater part of the fifty-odd miles to the French coast.

Fortunately, Marchi had no difficulty in landing us and we managed to get clear of the coast without having to answer any uncomfortable questions. That night we slept under a haystack, and the day following we parted company. Madasca felt that he would be safer on French soil, while I stuck to my determination to reach Spain. Two days later I was at Marseilles.

As, after my release from prison at the end of the War, I had returned to Corsica by way of Toulon, this was my first visit to Marseilles since that time Simone put the military authorities on to me. I kept a good lookout for her and Marie, not in the hope of renewing old friendships, but for fear they might recognize in André Spada André Gavini, deserter from the French army, and, putting two and two together with recent reports of trouble in Corsica, play me the same trick as before.

Marseilles, however, is a biggish town, and, as I searched the docks for a passage to Barcelona, I saw nothing of either girl.

My luck continued to hold good, for on the first day I fell in with the mate of the Marie Louise, of, I believe, La Rochelle, at a quayside café. One of the crew had fallen sick and, hearing I wanted to reach Barcelona, the mate offered me the spare berth, provided I was ready to ship that night. Nothing could have suited me better. The sooner I was out of Marseilles and away from France the better. I signed on under an assumed name, and twelve hours after having reached Marseilles I saw its lights dwindling behind us.

I had no definite plan in my mind. Once I had reached Barcelona I supposed that something would turn up. Barcelona is a busy city and there is generally work to be found there for a strong young man. Yes, I intended to work. It wasn't that my conscience was troubling me: and it was with no intention of "turning over a new leaf" that I had decided to start life anew in Barcelona. It was just that I was young and found plenty in life that made it worth living. Weren't the girls in Spain as pretty as any I might find in Marseilles? Or even, perhaps, Corsica for that matter? For I am afraid that old weakness of mine—a liking for a pair of bright eyes, glossy hair, a shapely figure—was still very much alive in spite of the three years I had spent in prison through Simone's betrayal of me. So it was with a pleasant feeling of expectation that I landed at Barcelona.

I have heard that I have been described in the newspapers as the "Bandit King of Lovers" and the "Brigand of a Thousand Loves." That, of course, is an exaggeration: it is a trick the journalists have of seizing upon some facet of a man's nature and stressing it for the sake of a good headline. But even allowing for journalistic exaggeration, there is no denying that women have been my one great weakness. I tell you this to explain Marita, although I did not meet her immediately upon my arrival at Barcelona.

For several weeks I hung about the town doing odd jobs of work. For a while I worked on the wharves, handling bales of wool. Tiring of this, I moved out to the olive groves. This was an occupation more to my liking. A town, to me, is a place where you may go for enjoyment—to a dance hall, to drink, to find women. Civilization, that is, the civilization of a big town or city, makes me feel uncomfortable. My eyes demand a horizon that is not bounded by a row of chimney pots or a string of cranes; my ears are deaf to the blaring of a motor horn, the wind in the Maquis is the music they like best; my nostrils have no use for petrol fumes, the scent of the wet earth is the perfume they seek. So I was glad to leave the city behind and find a place where my senses were not continually outraged.

From the little cottage the owner of the olive grove let me occupy, I could see the sun sink behind the heights of Tibidabo. Of course, it was nothing like my native Corsica, but it had its beauties. It was a relief to get out of the swarming city into the suburbs with their almost tropical vegetation. After the suburbs you come to the sloping hillsides with their vineyards and olive groves. Here you could forget the city with its dirt and noise.

The man for whom I worked—I have forgotten his name— was decent enough. He let me occupy a small cottage that was practically smothered in a purple climbing plant. Sometimes even now, eleven years after, I imagine at night that I can smell its sweet, suffocating fragrance.

I was happy there for a while. My work was light and my responsibilities were few. I had food, tobacco, shelter and the open air. I wanted but one thing—feminine companionship. I found this in Marita, my employer's daughter.

She was what I suppose the Americans would call "very beautiful, but very dumb." She was like a superb animal: big dark eyes, glossy black hair, an olive skin and a lovely body. She moved with the easy grace of the perfectly fit.

After the first few days I became conscious of her in the olive groves. She would come and, leaning against a tree, stand and watch me at my work. She was young—about seventeen—but as fully formed as an English or American girl of twenty-five. We people of the South mature early.

She never spoke to me. Just came and stood and watched. Presently I took to wishing her, "Good morning." When I spoke she flushed the color of a ripe plum, shuffled her feet uneasily, and presently drifted away. I found that if I did not appear to notice her she stayed longer, and, as her presence lent piquancy to my work, I pretended not to see her and contented myself with watching her out of the corner of my eye.

It was a funny companionship, Marita's and mine.

We hardly ever spoke. She was either dreadfully shy, or simple. Both, I believe; but her shyness was caused by her "dumbness." Not that I mean she was half-witted; rather she had that shy, dog-like simplicity of a wild animal. She was enormously interested in me and yet at the same time afraid. And, as with wild things, if you do not appear to take much notice of them, but carry on with your work, they come to look upon you as fairly harmless, bit by bit Marita seemed to lose her fear of me. She still spoke but little, and would flush and look startled if I spoke to her, nevertheless she would sit quite complacently watching me with her big dark eyes, which no longer were afraid to meet mine. It seemed sometimes to me, as I looked into those eyes, that there lurked an invitation in them. But if I looked too long into them she would lower her long black lashes or look away, so that I was never certain. Then one night I knew.

I had finished my supper and had gone out to smoke a cigar on the hillside. I have always loved the night. Sounds and scents, which mean so much to me, seem sharper then. It was late when I returned. As I neared my cottage I thought I detected a movement in the doorway beneath the deeper shadows cast by the climbing plant. Slip- ping my hand into my pocket, I drew out my gun, which I was never without. There was always at the back of my mind the possibility that the police might some day trace me.

On the alert, I advanced. I had not been mistaken. There was a human figure by my door.

I pointed my gun and called out sharply:

"Who's there? Stand out. I've got you covered."

At the same moment I side-stepped sharply, half-expecting to hear the spit of an automatic. Nothing happened, only there came a low, husky voice that said:

"Don't shoot, André. It's me — Marita."

She would not go. Perhaps I did not try hard enough to persuade her.

All my life I shall remember the scent of that purple plant that climbed out of my window — and remembering it, think of Marita.

The next morning I made an excuse to my employer and left the olive groves. I knew him as a quick-tempered man with the true Spaniard's fondness for his knife. Not that I was afraid of him, but I had no desire in those days for publicity. I could not have afforded it.

Indirectly, however, Marita brought me trouble, for it was through her that I returned to Barcelona, where almost immediately I was arrested and deported to Ajaccio to stand my trial for the murder of the gendarmes Antoine and Caillard.

VI

It puzzled me how the police had succeeded in tracing me to Barcelona. The more I thought about it the more certain I became that somebody had sold me to them. This was partly confirmed by one of my escort. Not that he said anything definite—rather it was by what he left unsaid that I got to know that my suspicion was correct.

Now only two people knew of my intention to hide in Barcelona—Stephano Madasca, my cousin, and Marchi. Of Madasca's loyalty I had no doubt. If I had needed any proof, he had given it to me that night we defended his cottage against the police. Then it was Marchi. With this realization there came a burning desire for revenge, and I registered an oath that if ever I should be free again I would kill Marchi.

Evidently news of my capture had reached Ajaccio well before my own arrival there, for on my way from the harbor to the gaol, groups of interested Corsicans appeared, and before we had gone far we had collected a largish crowd.

This was evidently not to the liking of the police, for after a few vain attempts to disperse the crowd, my escort closed in about me.

We were passing through some of the meaner streets of the town when I caught sight of Stephanini and Rutili amongst the crowd. With them were some of the more hotheaded young men from Lopigna.

It soon became clear that the crowd was getting out of hand. Put half a dozen trouble-seekers in a normally peaceable crowd and you have the ingredients of a first-class riot. It is mass psychology, and Stephanini and Rutili were working upon it for all they were worth.

Before long the crowd became so dense that my escort was brought to a standstill. Foolishly, perhaps, one of the police struck a man who jostled him. It was the match to the tinder. In a moment the narrow street was filled with the mob roar. Women screamed, men shouted, cursed and used their fists.

Over a gendarme's shoulder I saw Rutili signaling to me. Choosing my moment, I writhed free. One gendarme I caught behind the knees with the toe of my boot and saw him go under the feet of the mob; another I butted under the jaw with my forehead. The next moment I was wriggling and squirming my way through the crowd, Rutili at my side. At that moment I was glad of my lack of height; once clear of the police and I was swallowed up in the crowd where a man of more imposing stature might have stood out.

We were soon outside the crowd and, doubling down a side street, put as much distance between us and the police as we could in a short time.

As we ran, Rutili told me that he was lodging in a friend's house. The friend he could vouch for. There I would be safe until I could leave the town. Unobserved we arrived at the house of Rutili's friend, who, I believe, was called Marco, though I am not quite certain of this.

I was still wearing my handcuffs, but Rutili borrowed a file and freed me. Then we sat down with Marco to a meal, and, as we sat, I told them what had happened since we had last met.

Rutili looked across the table at me.

"So you suspect Marchi of having sold you?"

I nodded.

"I don't suspect," I told them. "I'm certain. Who else could have? Stephano Madasca would never have given me away to the police, besides which, they are hunting for him too. No, it is Marchi, for no one else knew that I intended making for Barcelona."

"And what do you intend to do about it?" asked Marco.

"Do about it?" I glanced across at Rutili. "What do you suppose I shall do?"

For answer Rutili smiled and laid his gun on the table.

"The police have taken your revolver, of course. Until we can get more, take one of mine. You will need it when you meet Marchi."

"And after that, what?" asked Marco.

I told him that I would never leave Corsica again. It was my intention to join Romanetti once I had settled with Marchi.

"And that should not be a long business," said Rutili, "for he is lodging in Ajaccio with relatives of mine. I know the house well—and the people. Poor swine, like Marchi."

Unobserved by us, a woman had come in and was watching us keenly. Rutili was the first to see her. He glanced up and said:

"Well, Madame Pinelli, so you see my friend has come to stay." Then to me: "This is Marco's mother, André."

The woman looked closely at me, nodded her head and went out again without speaking.

Later, when I was alone with Rutili, I asked:

"Do you think we are safe in this house? Marco seems all night. But that woman, his mother—"

Rutili shook his head.

"She is safe enough," he said. "She thinks much but says little. I do not think we have anything to fear from her."

That day Rutili made inquiries and returned to me in the afternoon to say that Marchi was still lodging with his relatives, a man named Pompa and his son.

"We had better wait until it is dark," he advised. "The police are still searching for you in a half-hearted way, though they believe that you have got clear of Ajaccio and taken to the Maquis. Here are two guns—no, you needn't pay for them—I didn't. I went to the gunsmith and was most particular in my choice. He must have had at least forty revolvers and automatics out on the counter for my inspection. It was very easy to slip two into my pocket when his back was turned. With so many on the counter he will never miss them. In the end I was not satisfied with what he had to show me and came away—with those."

He tapped the two guns on the table and I joined in his laughter.

It was dark when we left our lodgings, and I had little fear of being recognized by the police. As Rutili had said, they were probably only pretending to search for me for appearance's sake, believing that I had escaped into the Maquis.

Pompa's house was a little way outside the town, which was all to the good, for the sound of our firearms would attract less attention and we would have a better chance of escape once we had finished our business.

All the way to the cottage I thought of the vow I had made when I had realized that it was Marchi who had betrayed me. To a Northerner, I believe, my action would be looked upon as cold-blooded revenge—murder even: but to me it is incomprehensible that any man, who believes himself worthy of that title, can hold up his head amongst his fellow men if he does not obtain full satisfaction for his betrayal. Have you Britishers and Americans no spirit? If a man steals our women he does so with the knowledge that he is asking for a knife between his shoulder blades, or for a bullet. But you, you with a solicitor's letter, take your affair to the courts and parade it before the world. Perhaps, too, you claim damages from the thief, and he has to pay you a sum of money to make up to you for the loss of your wife. In Corsica we do not sell our women.

And so with Marchi's betrayal of me; I would not have felt myself a man if I had not accomplished my vendetta. When it is a question of honor, that question can only be settled between the two concerned. And so it was that my right hand itched for my gun as we approached Pompa's cottage.

It was a small place, huddled between some trees on the edge of a stretch of marshy ground. There was a cool wind blowing down from the hills, and for a moment I stood and listened to its voice amongst the leaves and smelled the old, familiar scents of the Maquis that it brought. Never till I die shall I lose that odd feeling of excitement when the wind comes down from Monte Rotondo, bringing with it the faint, indescribable scents of the Maquis.

There was a light in a back window of the cottage. From behind a bush Rutili and I peered into the room, where we could see three men seated at a table. Two I did not know, but the third, the one facing the window, I recognized immediately as Marchi. Rutili was for shooting him from where we stood. It was an easy shot, and safe; but I would not agree. I wanted Marchi to know who was at the other end of the gun that spat death at him. Only thus would I feel that my vendetta had been accomplished.

At that moment Marchi raised his head and I found myself gazing straight into his eyes. Had he seen me? I could not be certain. I imagined that it was too dark where we stood for him to be able to discern us; but a moment later, when he rose and left the room, I began to feel that I had made a mistake. Rutili confirmed my fears.

"Better rush them," he whispered. "I believe Marchi saw us and is going to bolt."

Throwing the door open, we burst into the cottage. The two men spun round in their chairs.

"Where's Marchi?" I barked.

"How should I know?" growled the elder man, whom I took to be Pompa. "He is not here."

There was no time to waste in talking as Marchi might already be out of the house and away into the marshes, so I pushed past and opened the door through which I had seen him pass. Rutili followed close on my heels. We were hardly through the doorway when something pinged past my head and embedded itself in the wall. At the same moment there came the crack of a revolver in the room behind us.

Rutili stopped, for I heard the crack of his gun and a shout of pain. There were more shots and the splintering of glass and woodwork. I did not wait, however, for Marchi was the game I hunted. Rutili, I felt, was safe enough, for he was shooting from the dark into the light.

There was an open door on the other side of the house, and as I blundered out through this into the open a bullet whizzed past me and, hitting a stone, ricocheted off into the darkness with a sound like a flying beetle.

I ducked back into the house just as Marchi's gun spat again, and the bullet flattened out against the wall not a foot from me. But this time I had seen the spurt of flame from Marchi's gun, and instantly I replied with mine—six shots in as good a circle as I could make around the spot at which I had seen the flame spit out.

For a moment there was silence. Then I detected the sound of running feet, faintly, for the wind was blowing from me to my quarry. At once I set off in pursuit, but the darkness and my lack of knowledge of the ground hindered me.

Presently I gave up the search in disgust. I was casting around for the spot from which Marchi had sniped me when Rutili joined me.

"Well?" he asked. "What luck?"

"None," I replied morosely. "What happened to your"

"Poor shots, Pompa and the lad. *N'importe*. Pompa will get no more shooting practice."

I knew what he meant. "And the youth?" I asked.

"Winged only. I took his gun and he is blubbering away in the back room. Poor cattle, these Pompas. Ah! Is this where Marchi was lying?"

He had struck a match and, shielding it with his hand, examined the ground.

"You hit him. See—blood, plenty of it. The man must have been bleeding like a pig. He won't get far tonight. Pity, though, that you did not shoot through the window. You would have made certain."

It was no use cursing, but curse I did. To have lived for these last weeks with this object in view—to kill Marchi—and then to have bungled it! It was almost more than I could bear.

"Never mind," consoled Rutili, "there is always a tomorrow. But now I think we had better return to my lodgings. I can hear voices. Our shots have been heard. *En avant, mon brave!*"

I was in an ill-temper the next day. I do not like bungling at any time, but most particularly when a man was living a life such as I was, it would inevitably lead to death. A man who lives by his wits and his gun cannot afford mistakes.

Rutili, however, was as cheerful as ever—he was a true lionheart was the "Lion of Lopigna."

"Why look so glum?" he wanted to know. "Marchi cannot possibly escape. Just lie here quietly and I shall make inquiries. News of our little affair will be all over the town today. I am certain to get some hint as to where Marchi has gone."

Moi, I was not so certain. Marchi had received a good shaking up the previous night, and if he had any sense, and I had no reason to doubt this, he would lie low for a while. I was not surprised, therefore, when Rutili returned at nightfall to say that so far he had been unsuccessful.

"But," he said, brightening up, "there is always a tomorrow."

"Oh, hold your tongue," I told him irritably. "Your *bon mots* make me feel sick."

In those days I had not learnt the virtue of patience. I was too eager, too headstrong. Later, under the leadership of Romanetti, I learnt how to wait for weeks, months even, with no sign of impatience, though the desire for action might be eating into me.

I was uncomfortable, too, about Marco and his mother—chiefly about the mother. I did not trust her, and my position was too delicate for me to be able to afford placing myself in the hands of anyone I did not trust. I spoke to Rutili again about it, but he laughed my misgivings aside.

"The old woman? She is all right. You need not fear. And as for Marco, he is a good friend."

I hoped he was right, but I still had my doubts.

It was late when Rutili returned that evening, and I was growing very impatient at waiting cooped up in the house, for I dared not venture out in the streets for fear of being recognized. But in a moment my impatience was forgotten, for I had only to glance at Rutili's excited face to know that he had news. I followed him into his room and closed the door.

"Well?" I demanded.

"I have traced him—the slug! He has crawled to hide in the house of a man named Sena. Tonight we shall make no mistake."

I asked him how many men we were likely to have to contend with if, as in the case of the Pompas, they decided to protect the fugitive.

"There is only Sena," said Rutili, "and his wife and two sons. They are mere youths. Jean, I believe, is only eighteen, and Francois thirteen. Besides which, we shall have Dominique Ettori with us."

"Ettori? ' I asked. '"Who is he? I don't know him."

"He is a good friend. It was through him that I learnt where Marchi had hidden. He has an old score to wipe off against Sena and asked if he might come with us."

"*Mais certainement,*" I agreed. "When do we start?"

"Ettori will call for us. It won't be long now. But first I must eat."

Two hours later we were entering a small café in a back street.

A lad of about eighteen came forward and asked what we wanted. Rutili gave an order for a bottle of red wine and some meat sandwiches.

"That was Jean Sena," I told myself.

No sooner was he out of the room than Ettori silently locked the street door.

Half a dozen strides carried me into the back portion of the café.

"You, Rutili, guard the back door," I snapped. "Ettori, look to the foot of the stairs whilst I search these rooms."

At the sound of my voice Jean Sena came out of the kitchen and asked if I wanted anything.

I told him I did. I wanted Marchi, the man who was lodging with them. He turned very white and, not taking his eyes off my gun, backed into the kitchen. I followed him, and seeing a large open cupboard without a window, I ordered him into it, locking the door upon him.

"If you shout," I warned him, "I shall drill holes in the panel of that door with my gun. Understand?"

I heard a muffled, *"Oui, monsieur."*

The rest of the ground-floor rooms drew blank.

"Rutili," I called, "watch our retreat. Ettor1 and I are about to try the next floor."

We were half-way up the stairs when a figure appeared at the head of them. There was a rifle in his hand.

"What do you want?" he demanded.

"Out of the way," I shouted. "I don't want you. I want Marchi."

The muzzle of the rifle moved up, and my finger tightened on my trigger. But before I could shoot there came from behind me the crack of Ettori's revolver.

Sena gave a loud cry, "Ettori!" and toppled forward down the stairs, almost carrying me with him in his fall.

As I bounded to the head of the stairs a woman on the landing began to scream. Behind her was the younger Sena boy, a large poker in his hand.

"Drop that thing, child," I ordered him.

He looked at first as though he would disobey, but when the muzzle of my gun swung round and pointed directly at him the poker fell with a clatter.

"Ettori, guard these two. And if that woman makes any more noise, gag her."

Quickly I went through the rooms. There was not a moment to lose if we wanted to get away with safe hides. No doubt already the shot had been heard and some busybody had run for the police. Each room, however, was empty till I came to the one over the café, the front room overlooking the street. This was locked.

If Marchi was there it would be useless to call to him to open, so I put my shoulder to the door, but it was solidly made and refused to budge.

I had drawn back to get a shot at the lock when there came a dull report, and a large splinter suddenly jerked out of the door frame within a few inches of my face.

J jumped aside, and putting the angle of the wall between me and Marchi's fire, I shot out the lock. A good kick sent the door crashing open.

The room was empty!

I have never crossed a room quicker in my life than I crossed that room to the open window. I looked down into the street and the blood hummed triumphantly in my veins. Not ten yards away and running fast was a man. His left arm was in a sling. So much I could see in the light of a street lamp—and then I fired. The figure jerked forward and went on running. Its one arm was thrown up. And as it ran the body seemed to be going too fast for the legs. It was leaning forward, farther and farther. Then it hit the ground, turned a somersault and came to rest, sprawled out in the gutter. Suddenly I laughed. I was reminded of a puppet show. I was the showman, the café window was the flies, the street was the stage, and Marchi the puppet. I had released the string: the puppet had crumpled up upon its little stage.

Behind me on the landing Ettori called impatiently.

"Come along, in there! Even if you don't value your skin, I value mine."

Ettori was right. Before long the police would arrive. Regretfully I turned my back on my puppet stage. The figure in the gutter had not moved. It lay in a pool of yellow lamplight, its face turned up to the night sky.

"And so," I muttered to myself, "may all die who betray André Spada."

VII

We reached our lodgings without mishap, and, very well pleased with our night's work, I turned in to sleep.

First of all, however, we talked over our future arrangements. We had parted company with Ettori, who seemed to be suffering from an attack of cold feet. At the time, he had been brave enough, but now that the business was over he had begun to feel the reaction. Perhaps it was because he was so much older than we were. We had hot young blood in our veins to warm our courage when there was no longer the stimulus of direct action.

He stood for a moment fiddling nervously with his belt.

"I should have shot those two boys," he said, "and the old woman, too. It would have been safer."

"But why?" I asked, a little contemptuously.

He gave a little shiver.

"When you were in that front room settling with Marchi and I was on the landing guarding Sena's woman and the boy, she cursed me. No, my friend, you needn't laugh. I am not so superstitious as you think. I know that woman. Never so long as she lives will she be content until she has had her revenge. She will bring up her sons with but one passion in their hearts—to kill me, too. Yes, I was a fool not to make an end of them all."

Rutili and I laughed at him for a nervous old fool, but how truly he had judged the woman was proved by something that happened in a café in Nice ten years later.

As we turned in, Rutili said:

"Tomorrow night we shall join Romanetti. It will be safer than this pestilential town."

But the gods evidently had other plans, for the following morning Rutili woke me with the news that the house was surrounded by police.

"A minute ago," he said, "I looked out and saw Marco's mother talking to a *brigadier de police* and pointing up at this window. André, you were right about that woman. If I had listened to you we wouldn't be here with those damned police waiting to shoot us down."

"When you've had as much experience with women as I have, my friend," I told him, "you'll know when they are to be trusted and when they are not."

Which just shows how ignorant I was of women myself, or I wouldn't be where I am now—watching a patch of grey sky through a row of iron bars.

It was evident that we were in as tight a position as we had ever been—or were ever likely to be.

After a quick consultation, it was decided that Rutili should guard the front of the house and I the rear.

Fortunately, the previous night, I had had the sense to confiscate Sena's rifle and several boxes of his ammunition. I was glad to have it, for a rifle is a far better weapon for sniping through windows than either a revolver or automatic: you present a smaller target to the attacker.

I saw, however, that both my guns were filled and the safety catches raised; then, slipping a clip into Sena's carbine, I chose what seemed to be the best position from which to shoot. The house at this point jutted out. It was too small to call it a wing— two rooms, one above the other, about fifteen feet in length. The window I had decided upon was small and deeply recessed, and, since it was at an angle to the main building, I commanded the entire back of the house, door and windows.

There was a narrow lane at this side of the house bounded on the other side by a high bank overgrown with shrub. I was considering the possibility of leaping from the main window of the room that looked out upon this bank when one of the police showed his head around the corner.

Zip! His *kepi* flew off and he quickly withdrew his head. I patted Sena's carbine. A good, true implement. One I could trust.

The bark of Rutili's gun came from the front room — again and then again.

"What luck?" I shouted.

"Winged one," was Rutili's laconic reply.

After my first shot I saw no more of the police at the back of the house. They evidently realized that I had it too well covered for them to risk coming out into the open.

Still keeping my eye on the lane, I turned my attention again to the bank. Opposite the back door there was a gap of about twenty feet to the bank. Therefore, provided nothing funny happened on the portion that was out of sight, the gap opposite the end window should not be more than about five feet.

Risking leaving my lookout for a moment, I ran to the back window. Sure enough, only a narrow gap separated me from the cliff face. And what was more, there was a moderately good foothold on its side and a sturdy-looking bush for a hand-hold.

I ran back to my side window and was just in time to see one of the police making for the back door. I took a snap shot and had the satisfaction of seeing him drop his carbine and topple in through the doorway.

He was only wounded, I believed, but for the time being he was out of action.

Now was the time, I felt, to make our getaway, before the police thought of occupying the cliff, either as a vantage-point of attack or in order to cut off our retreat.

I called to Rutili and told him what I proposed to do.

The lane was still clear. I ran to the end window and opened the casement wide. To the right of me in the lane, and, naturally, screened from my other window, was a *brigadier* of police and a handful of men.

They heard me open the window and a spatter of bullets flew past my head, several shattering the glass of the open window. Dropping to the sill, I nestled my carbine into a corner of the windowframe and drew a bead on the *brigadier*. It meant shooting left-handedly, but that has never troubled me. The shot went home and the *brigadier* made way for promotion in the local police force.

In a moment the lane was clear, and, having judged the distance to an inch, I braced myself and jumped. The side of the cliff leapt forward to meet me. My free hand clutched at the friendly tree.

I was across.

"Rutili!" I roared.

"*En un moment!*" he called back. "I have just one more thing to do."

I heard him cross the front room at a run, then—the fool!—I heard the clatter of his feet on the stairs. He was descending into the house.

"Rutili!"

"*Un moment!*"

There came the splintering of a door, a woman's shriek, a volley of shots; then Rutili's steps pounding up the stairs again. A *kepi* poked cautiously around the corner of the house; my carbine spat and the *kepi* jerked back. Rutili appeared at the window.

"Where the hell did you go?" I snapped.

"To settle a score, mon ami. Marco is dead and the old hag, if she lives, will remember Rutili all her life."

"*C'est bon.* Now jump."

Rutili gauged the distance with his eye, crouched, and sprang. His feet rattled on the side of the bank. A *kepi* appeared at both corners of the house. On the point of leaning forward to give a hand to Rutili, I stepped back and my carbine spat again, to the right, to the left. The heads ducked back.

Out of the corner of my eye I saw Rutili's hands clawing the air. He was slipping back. Stones rattled down on to the cobbles of the lane. I was too late to catch him. Sliding and bumping, he went down the steep side of the bank, his arms and legs spread out in a futile effort to save himself. With a clatter he hit the lane. A volley of oaths told me that, at least, he was alive. But he was like a rat in a trap. The bank was too steep for him to climb. Each end of the lane was occupied by police and, probably by now, the house, too.

From where I stood, about fifteen feet from the ground, the almost perpendicular sides of the cliff eased off, making ascent easy enough. Still keeping the lane covered, I retreated a little way up the hillside until I found some largish boulders that would give me protection.

What I had feared very soon happened. A rifle muzzle appeared at the window from which I had jumped. Rutili was entirely surrounded, and, so long as that rifle covered the cliff side, I was powerless to help him.

I hated the idea of leaving Zetto Rutili, but it would have been madness to attempt rescue. My first movement down the cliffside would have called forth a bullet from that window. Alive and free, I would be of more help than if I were dead or in the hands of the police.

Even now they might be drawing a cordon round me. If I were to escape I could not afford to wait. So with a heavy heart I wormed my way up the hillside to safety.

Ajaccio was now no longer even moderately safe for me. In fact, it would be definitely unhealthy for me to stay there. With Rutili in the hands of the police I had no *pied-à-terre*. I took to the Maquis.

It had been my intention for some time to join Romanetti, but, until I was satisfied about Rutili's safety, I did not feel free to leave the district.

There was now only one of us four friends still free—Santu Stephanini. Ferrari had joined Romanetti, Rutili was in prison, and I was an outlaw. There only remained Stephanini upon whom I could rely to help me in obtaining Rutili's release. In search of him, I made my way through the Maquis to Lopigna, and that night presented myself at his house.

He was delighted to see me, though he was not surprised. News of the last few days' happenings, ending in Rutili's arrest, had reached Lopigna, and little else was talked of in the cafés and streets.

Stephanini was one of the hardest cases I had ever met—five years in Fresne Gaol is not calculated to soften a man—but there was a gleam of admiration in his eyes as he said:

"You know, André, you have a reputation. It is said of you that you are the greatest killer in the whole of Corsica—greater than Romanetti even—far greater than Caviglioli or Bartoli."

It was one of the proudest moments of my life when I heard Stephanini link my name with those of the three great bandit chiefs of Corsica. Romanetti I have spoken of already. The others, Caviglioli and Bartoli, each had their band of followers, but they existed only on Romanetti's sufferance. So long as they left the King of the Maquis in peace and did not poach on his preserves, he was content to acknowledge their rights to certain portions of the island. At times, even, he found them useful, when concerted action was needed. For their part, they went in fear of Romanetti and acknowledged him as King of the Maquis.

"One day," said Stephanini, "we shall see André Spada as King of the Maquis."

I did not tell him that if I realized my ambition I would be. Instead, I began to plan how we might rescue Rutili.

"It is useless to attempt force. If he were in the *Poste de Police* at Lopigna—yes; in Ajaccio Gaol—no. If it weren't so, I would go to Romanetti and get his help."

Stephanini agreed.

"But what," he asked, "can you hope to do?"

"Naturally there will be a trial and witnesses will be called. If we can only obtain the names of the witnesses who are to appear for the police we may be able to silence them. They have seen what has happened to others who fought against me—if they are wise they will take your hint and hold their tongues at the trial."

Stephanini grinned broadly.

"*Hein?* Then I am to intimidate them? You seem to expect us all to dance to your piping. However, as you can't very well go to Ajaccio, I will; and if I can't silence their tongues for you, nobody can."

So the following day Stephanini went to Ajaccio and it was a whole week before I saw him again.

Every night for that week I had called at his house, but no light burned in his windows and I knew that he could not have returned.

When at length I saw the light of his lamp making an orange oblong in the darkness, I almost broke his door down in my eagerness.

"*Dîtes-moi,*" I demanded. '"How did things go in Ajaccio? Have you fixed the witnesses?"

Stephanini crossed to the cupboard and brought out a bottle and two glasses.

"Not so fast, André. You are as impetuous as a boy in love. Yes, I have arranged things. I do not think many of the witnesses will dare open their mouths at the trial."

I rubbed my hands together and stamped to my feet, upsetting my chair.

"*C'est bon,*" I cried, "Rutili will be acquitted. If there are no witnesses he cannot be convicted. When is the trial to be?"

"Wednesday, next week."

"You will attend, of course, and bring me news as quickly as possible?"

Stephanini said that he would.

How my patience held out for the following week I do not know. I always have been essentially a man of action; this waiting tried me very hard. If there was anything I could have done, done it would have been. But with Rutili safely locked away in Ajaccio Gaol I was absolutely powerless to help. I could only wait, and urge Stephanini on in his efforts to silence the leading witnesses. In the hope that it would bear more weight than Stephanini's words, I wrote to some, Stephanini delivering my notes.

At last the day came, and, with Stephanini, I set out for Ajaccio. I arranged with him that I would wait in the Maquis as near to the town as was safe. As soon as the trial was over he was to join me and let me know how things had gone.

Slowly the day dragged out. The sun climbed up over the mountains behind me and declined towards the sea.

Below me lay Ajaccio, spread out about its harbor, its white houses gleaming in the bright sunlight.

I grew stiff, for I hardly moved, and my food lay untouched by my side.

Then at last, when the sun had gone and a soft breeze was creeping down from the cooling Maquis to the sea, Stephanini came.

He sat down by me and, in his deliberate way, lighted a cigarette before he spoke.

"Well?" I asked sharply.

He blew out the match and looked across at me.

"André," he said, "do you know that you are a power that is making itself felt in Corsica?"

I asked him what he meant.

"There has never been a stranger trial in Ajaccio. A foreigner would have laughed: the police nearly wept. Witness after witness was called into the box. Some were quite dumb, and others, suddenly deaf or idiots. The police argued with them, even threatened them, but they had lost their memories. It was rather a pitiful sight—the sweat was pouring down their faces—"

"Oh, damn the witnesses," I cut in. "What about Rutili? What was the verdict?"

For a while Stephanini was silent. His cigarette had gone out and before replying he lit another.

At our feet the lights of Ajaccio were winking into life.

The breeze had dropped. It was very still. A steamer, groping its way out of the harbor, hooted dismally.

"The verdict?" said Stephanini. "Guilty! Rutili is to go to the guillotine."

VIII

So I had failed. All my planning and scheming had come to nothing. Rutili was to go to the guillotine and nothing that I could do now would save him.

In that moment I realized the cruelty of "civilization." Its way was so unlike the clean, swift justice of the Maquis. In our vendettas a man wrongs you and, later, you kill him — or he kills you. He has his fighting chance. What justice is there in an order of things that first tortures, then murders its victims?

Think of the torture of the trial, and the waiting — both before and after. Finally the murder. What chance has a man of defending himself once he has fallen into the clutches of the law? He is condemned. He is bound. His head is placed on a block. The blade falls — zutt! Like that.

Dio mio! And they call that justice. In the Maquis a man dies like a man, with a gun in his hand and a sporting chance of defending himself.

The justice of civilization is farther from the justice of the banditti than the slaughterhouse is from *la chasse,* where the animal has, at least, a sporting chance of going free or even killing its pursuer.

It was then, as I sat looking down at the lights of Ajaccio spread out at my feet like a jeweled carpet, that I realized how final was my break with civilization. Never more, whatever happened, would I like its houses and submit myself to its petty laws and arbitrary injustice. From now on the Maquis would be my home and my refuge.

At length Stephanini spoke.

"I am sorry, André. We did what we could. And now?"

I lifted my head from my cupped palms. It was like lifting myself back form the grave, so deeply was I sunken in my thoughts.

"Now?" I said dully. "Why, I shall go to Romanetti—as he asked me to do. Even if I could I would never return to—that!"

I threw my hand out towards the lights of Ajaccio.

Stephanini nodded. Presently he rose and stretched himself, so that his long arms seemed almost to reach up to the stars— they hang so low above the Mediterranean.

"Ah, well. I shall not come with you—yet. Some day, perhaps. *Addio!*"

He was gone and I was alone with my thoughts.

With the dropping of the wind a great stillness had fallen. A crane rattled, the sound reaching me clearly in the still air. Somewhere nearer a guitar awoke, its notes plucking at my heart as the player plucked his strings. As always, it reminded me of the soft laughter of women, their cool hands, the lights that danced in their dark eyes. Was I to leave all that, too? I sat thinking of Maria, of Simone and of Marita, the thought of whom brought back the hot scent of that purple creeping plant.

Gradually the lights winked out till but a sprinkling marked the streets and wharves. Still that guitar thrummed on, speaking of the one thing that civilization could give me that perhaps the Maquis might not offer. At last it was silent.

A night bird cried as it swept down the hillside. The surge of the sea came faintly, but never ceasing, to my ears.

At length, as the sky above Monte Rotondo was graying, driving the stars before it, I rose and eased my cramped limbs.

I had done with civilization. Today I would seek out Romanetti.

This time I did not ask the help of Giocundi, the woodcutter. I had once visited the mountain camp of Romanetti! I could find it again. Or so I thought. No man, unless he has seen the Maquis in all its primeval wildness, can believe how almost impenetrable its thickets are. Paths are few and every now and then one's way is barred by deep ravines scoured out of the mountainside by streams, eagerly hungering for the sea.

All day I wandered, as nearly lost as it was possible to be. No wonder the police had always found it impossible to dislodge the banditti from the Maquis. On all sides of me as I passed through the thick undergrowth were the most perfect ambuscades from which a man might shoot and never be seen.

It was towards evening a sharp challenge rang out from behind a clump of stunted oak.

"*Holà*, there! Where are you going?"

A man came out into the open carrying a carbine at the ready. He wore a red handkerchief knotted about his head. There was several days' black stubble on his chin. I turned to face him. At sight of my features he lowered his gun.

"Spada!" he cried.

"You remember me?"

"Yes, you came some months ago to visit Nonce Romanetti. He will be glad to see you. We have had news of the happenings in Ajaccio these last few days."

I could not have been so far out in my direction, though I had begun to despair of finding Romanetti's camp, for half an hour later we came upon the track I remembered from my last visit.

Looking back it seems strange to me that I had so much difficulty in finding the camp, for as time passed, I grew to know the Green Palace—a name by which the Maquis was sometimes known—as well as any farmer knows his fields.[5]

---

[5] "June in Corsica is the month when the bandit's title for the Maquis, '*Le Palais Vert*' (The Green Palace), best describes the perfumed wilderness of aromatic plants, thorny scrub, and larch forests of which Napoleon writes in his memoirs – that if he were passing his island far out at sea he would know it by the scent, even if the island were invisible." Edith Halford Nelson, "Adventure in Corsica with the Bandit André Spada," from *Out of the Silence* (London: Rider and Co., 1944), pp. 76.

There was real pleasure in Romanetti's face as he held out his hand to me on our arrival.

"I knew that one day you would come," he said simply.

At the time I did not know it, but later I realized that he was feeling the strain of his leadership. He was in need of a trusted lieutenant who, besides being fearless, could be relied upon to lead men. The members of his band were tough and brave, but, without exception, they lacked the power of generalship.

Romanetti was one of the best judges of men I have ever met, and I do not think that I am unduly sounding my own trumpet when I say that in me Romanetti saw an ideal right-hand man, a possible successor to himself should anything happen to him.

It is true that his opinion was greatly influenced by the reports that had reached him of my affairs in Ajaccio during the last few days; to them I owed much of my prestige amongst the banditti. Almost immediately upon my enrollment in Romanetti's band I was tacitly accepted as the second-in-command. At first this fact surprised me a little. I had come with the determination of making my influence felt: but I had expected opposition, jealousy upon the part of others who had served under Romanetti for several years, and who, not unnaturally, would demand preferential treatment. However, there was none. Evidently I was looked upon as an experienced and determined killer whose judgment and wit could be relied upon; and I was treated accordingly.

Thus, within six months of that fateful shot in the Café Marguerite, I found myself the acknowledged lieutenant of Romanetti, the King of the Maquis.

IX

The more I saw of Romanetti, the more deeply I grew to admire him. There was something very great about him; it was evident, not only in his courage and his almost uncanny wisdom, but in the generosity and chivalry of his nature.

It was not long after I joined him that there happened something that showed all these characteristics of his with great clearness.

I had always known that Romanetti had a very effective spy service throughout the island, but I had never realized the extent of this network of espionage. And it was as perfect as it was extensive. It was built[,] to a great extent, upon Romanetti's system of bounty. The rich paid him well for his protection: he, in his turn, paid the peasantry well for keeping him advised of any items of news that might hold interest for him. It was a good system. The merchants, hotelkeepers, shopkeepers were assured of immunity—the poor had their pockets nicely lined, and Romanetti was able to move about in reasonable safety.

One day Romanetti called me into his room.

"We are about to have some amusement, my friend," he said. "' One of my informers has arrived to tell me that a certain young captain at the barracks has been making foolish boasts in the Mess. Perhaps he was a little drunk—who knows? At any rate, he says that the police of Corsica are a lot of incompetent fools, and that they go about the efforts to capture me in entirely the wrong way."

"The Captain knows a better way?" I suggested.

"Of course! He says that they will never catch me by sending out a posse of police or the military. One man alone should come and bring me back alive. It is a great scheme."

I laughed. The idea of a lone man going out into the Maquis and bringing back its king amused me.

"And is our friend the Captain prepared to test his plan?" I asked.

Romanetti nodded.

"*Mais oui*. His fellow officers dared him to make the attempt and he was in honor bound to agree to do so, unless he cared to be labeled a windbag by his friends. It will be an amusing game that we shall have with the brave Captain. What do you say, Spada? What will be his first move?"

I thought for a moment.

"He will not attempt to find you here," I decided. "He will want to have you nearer his own territory. No doubt he will send a messenger asking for an interview upon some trumped-up excuse, and request a meeting place nearer to Ajaccio."

Romanetti agreed. The following day proved my guess to be materially correct.

A messenger arrived at our camp and asked to speak with Romanetti. The gist of the message was that *le Capitaine Fournier* was exceedingly anxious to see Romanetti upon a very important matter, and, as his duties in Ajaccio did not permit of his making the journey to Romanetti's camp, would Romanetti arrange a meeting place nearer to Ajaccio? If the bandit chief would send a guide the Captain would accompany him alone.

Romanetti pretended to ponder the idea, although I knew that he had already decided to agree to the Captain's request. At length he said:

"Very well. Tell *le Capitaine Fournier* that at the next new moon I shall send a guide to bring *le Capitaine* to me. But understand, *le Capitaine* must come alone."

When the messenger was gone Romanetti turned to me.

"So you were right, Spada[!] Now I wonder what tricks *Monsieur le Capitaine* will try. He can hardly hope to carry me back in his pocket."

It wanted about a week to the new moon; during this time Romanetti made his preparations. He chose the house of a friend not far from Ajaccio, and arranged about posting his guards for the night of the meeting. He also sent to Ajaccio for a detailed description of Captain Fournier.

"Who can tell," he said, "that our friend will come in person? He has probably some trick in his mind that he intends to try upon me. It is as well to be prepared."

At length the day arrived and Romanetti, having first received his spies' report that the way was clear, set out for the house he had chosen for the meeting, accompanied by me and a dozen of the bandits.

Soon after my enrollment with Romanetti I had been supplied with a horse: without one some of the journeys we had to make would have been impossible on account of the vast area of the Maquis. They were splendid animals, these horses of the banditti, rivaling the Italian cavalry in their dexterity over the difficult mountain country.

A little after dusk we arrived at the house, the guide was dispatched to Ajaccio, sentries were posted in well-concealed spots, and the room where Romanetti was to meet the Captain chosen.

Presently news arrived that the guide was returning with *le Capitaine Fournier*. A few minutes later another spy arrived.

"*Ce n'est pas le Capitaine Fournier lui-même*," he cried excitedly.

"I did not expect it would be," said Romanetti quite calmly. " Now what, I wonder, does our young friend intend to do?"

When the officer arrived, Romanetti gave no sign that he knew of the impersonation, but greeted him as though he were Captain Fournier.

The Corsican banditti pride themselves upon their hospitality and, according to custom, an elaborate meal had been prepared, with which was served some of the choicest wines that were to be found in Corsica.

The young officer ate, drank and talked, finally departing without giving any very satisfactory reason for his request for an interview. As soon as he had mounted his horse and the sound of its hoofs had died away, Romanetti turned to me.

"Now we can expect the fireworks to begin. Turn out the light, Spada."

He seated himself at a table at the end of the room facing the windows, so that anyone entering would stand out silhouetted against their grayness whilst he, himself, would be in absolute darkness. On the table in front of him he laid his two revolvers, fully loaded.

Moi, I took up my position in a corner where the breast of the fireplace, jutting out, formed some protection.

We had not long to wait. Suddenly the door burst open and a figure entered quickly, fastening the door behind him. From where we waited we could see his outline, a dark blur against the lighter background of the windows.

"Romanetti!" he cried. "I have you covered. In the name of the President of the French Republic I demand that you come quietly with me to Ajaccio. Your house is surrounded by the police. If you are wise you will surrender."

At this piece of bluff Romanetti laughed loudly. The Captain could not have Romanetti covered with his revolver unless by sheer chance, as the bandit chief must have been entirely invisible to him. And as for the house being surrounded by police—no wonder Romanetti laughed.

"And if you, *Monsieur le Capitaine Fournier*, are wise," he said softly, "you will go quietly back to your comrades in Ajaccio. You are young. You have your career before you. You do not wish to die yet."

Possibly the Captain felt he was being treated like a child; or he may have been shaken by the very different kind of reception from what he had expected. At any rate, he let out a burst of shots in Romanetti's direction. Fortunately, however, none found their mark.

In the silence that followed I heard the rattle of Romanetti's guns on the table. When he spoke the softness had gone out of his voice.

"*Monsieur le Capitaine,*" he said grimly, "your youth shows itself in your rashness. Why do you wish to kill me? I have never harmed you. Go, before it is too late. Romanetti is not anxious to kill men—but when they attack him—"

Captain Fournier gave a cry of rage. This common bandit, whom he had boasted that he would bring back alive, treated him as though he were a small boy. He saw no generosity in the bandit's speech; only an attempt to humiliate him. Again his revolver swept the end of the room from which Romanetti's voice had come.

This time the flash and crack of Romanetti's gun answered him. With hardly a sound he fell where he stood.

"Light that lamp, Spada," Romanetti called.

I came out from my retreat and did as he requested.

Captain Fournier lay in a heap before the window, one arm thrown out, the other crumpled under him. There was an expression of puzzled surprise on his young face.

Romanetti stood over his still body, looking down at him. He seemed little more than a lad, lying there: his fair wisp of moustache detracted from, rather than added to, his age. He was dressed in peasant's clothing, but that could not hide the stamp of the officer class.

"Poor boy!" said Romanetti. "I hated having to shoot him, but what would you? I gave him fair warning."

Seating himself on the edge of the table he ejected the cartridge from his revolver and began to clean the barrel.

"You see his plan, Spada? A poor one. He sends a brother officer to me believing that I shall be foolish enough to be deceived. Then, in his peasant's garb, he follows, waits till my interview with the supposed Capitaine Fournier is over, and, expecting to find me off my guard, bursts in upon us. It was childish. Do these poor military believe that we sleep?"

He shook his head sadly, shut one eye and squinted down the barrel of his gun.

"And what do we do with him?" I asked, jerking my head in the direction of the dead officer.

"He will have to be buried," decided Romanetti. "Call three of the men to bring a mule and some shovels. Tell them to make a decent job of it, mark the spot and inform his regiment."

Then he went out; but first he stood a few moments staring down regretfully at the rash young officer's body.

He was like that, was Romanetti. Never a murderer, hardly a killer even, and even when he did kill it was in self-defense and with much subsequent regret.

To me it seemed a sign of weakness, this regret of his. When you kill a man in fair fight, when it is a question of his life or yours, what is there to regret?

If a man killed me in fair fight I would not expect him to weep over my dead body. Why, then, should I weep over his?

Poor Romanetti! In many ways he was a dreamer, an idealist, but there was no denying that, with it all, he was a very great leader and a brave man.

X

Some people may wonder from what sources we bandits obtained our revenue. And, no doubt, suppose that the greater part of it came from robbery and pillage. This was not the case; at least not so far as the bigger bands were concerned.

The smaller bands did draw most of their livelihood from robbery, and it is this fact that gave the bigger gangs, such as Romanetti's, their power and an easy source of income.

The smaller bands, seeing some shopkeeper apparently making a tidy profit, would levy a toll upon him, failing the paying of which his place would be ransacked and possibly burned.

These were not our methods. We acted almost in the capacity of an insurance company. In return for an agreed sum of money, we gave our protection to the various shopkeepers, hotelkeepers and businessmen. So great was the power of Romanetti's band, that once a shopkeeper had paid his toll to Romanetti and come under our protection, the lesser bands never dared to molest him.

It was for this reason that Romanetti never tried to stamp out the small fry in the Maquis. The greater their depredations, the larger sums people were prepared to pay for our protection. It was a safe and easy, even lawful method of obtaining a regular revenue. If the smaller bands had been exterminated, then the only toll the shopkeepers would have paid would have been to insure themselves against ourselves. The other was a far better way. Not only did Romanetti refrain from stamping out the smaller bands, he even, when danger threatened them, co-operated in resisting the police or military.

A large revenue was absolutely essential to us bandits. Not so much for our food and clothing, but for distribution amongst the peasants. During his "reign," Romanetti must have distributed hundreds of thousands of francs throughout the island. It was not high-mindedness that caused him to do it, although I must say he was an exceedingly generous, even soft-hearted man.

That the money he poured out went to help those who needed it most was a real pleasure to him; but, after all, it was not the major consideration. Our own protection came first. While large sums were passing through our hands to the poorer classes, we were assured of a perfect spy service whose network spread to every corner of the island. No peasant wished to see his golden stream cut off at its source. They were, therefore, always on the alert for any news that might affect Romanetti's safety. There was also always the chance that a useful piece of information about the movements or plans of the authorities would produce a substantial bonus.

Another, and lesser, source of income was the mail route from Ajaccio to Lopigna. This route passed through some very lonely parts of the Maquis, following the trail upon which I had shot the two gendarmes when I rescued Ferrari.

But there was rarely anything of much value to be obtained from the mailbags and, unless we had received information that the mail coach was worth stopping, we left it alone.

One day, however, we conceived a plan by which the mail route could be made to produce a safe and regular revenue.

First we carried out a number of raids upon the coach. We gained little of value from these, but it was only a gesture to the postal authorities to show them what we could do. Next we sent a messenger to the postmaster at Ajaccio and offered to supply a driver and escort for the coach, and guarantee the safe transit of the mails. Our offer was accepted, and for nine months the mails travelled from Ajaccio to Lopigna and back again under our protection. It says a lot for Romanetti's word of honor and the authorities' trust in it that during that time, no matter how valuable the mails were, there was no complaint.

It was a French journalist on holiday in Corsica who was the cause of our losing this "contract." To him it seemed a remarkable thing that the mails were entrusted to a band of brigands for their transit. On his return to Paris he wrote an article upon the matter which was published and duly came to the eye of the authorities.

An arrangement like that can be winked at by the local authorities, but when it is given prominence in the newspapers, the higher authorities in France feel that something must be done to save their faces. A peremptory order was sent to Ajaccio to terminate the agreement.

It surprised me when Romanetti quite calmly received the news that we could no longer be allowed to carry the mail.

"Tomorrow morning," I told him, "I shall arrange an ambush, and we shall burn the mails and the coach."

But Romanetti shook his head decisively.

"No, Spada. It would mean bloodshed. At present we are living in peace with the authorities. Our subsidies are bringing in sufficient. Why stir up trouble?"

Grudgingly I had to agree as I dare not risk offending Romanetti.

"One day I may be in his place," I told myself. "Then we shall see. The postal authorities shall either let me carry those mails — or there will be no mails to carry."

There was another possible source of income, but we all were agreed in refraining from tapping it. That was the foreign tourists. They would have been a rich and easy prey, but an attack upon them would have meant inevitable trouble. As it was, much of their money passed to our pockets through the hands of the hotelkeepers and shopmen. With this we had to be content. For their part the tourists were attracted to the island by the glamour of the banditti, and it was an unwritten law amongst all the bands that tourists were to be given the freedom of the Maquis.

It was the breaking of this law by Caviglioli and Bartoli that caused the disruption of all the bands save mine.

I remember one occasion when some members of Caviglioli's band disregarded this law of the Maquis, and, had it not been for Romanetti's intervention, there would have been serious trouble. In all probability the French Government would have sent a punitive expedition, which was a thing that none of us wanted.

It was a little while after we had lost the contract for the carrying of the mails. Romanetti and I were riding through the Maquis with a small escort when we were startled by hearing screams for help. Romanetti swung his horse in amongst the trees with me following close on his heels. After a short canter we came out upon a clearing in the woods.

In the centre of the clearing was an abandoned motorcar. Judging by the sounds, its occupants were in trouble in the woods on the farther side.

Thrusting our way amongst the shrub, we came up with a number of Caviglioli's band hustling a man along. With them was a remarkably pretty girl who was, presumably, the man's daughter.

Here was a flagrant violation of one of the strictest laws of the Maquis, for these two were obviously tourists; American, I judged.

At sight of them Romanetti reined in, at the same time letting out such a flood of invective at Caviglioli's men that I felt glad that there was little chance of the girl understanding what he was saying.

For a moment the men stood doubtfully looking at one another, at a loss to know what to do. Evidently the capture of the American had been carried out with Caviglioli's consent, or, possibly, at his orders, with a view to ransom. Now here was Romanetti ordering them to release their captives. Which was better? To risk the anger of their leader or of the King of the Maquis?

However, Romanetti decided the matter for them. Drawing his guns, he threatened to shoot any man who was within range by the time he had counted ten.

"*Un—deux—*"

Some of the men looked defiant.

"*Trois—quatre—*"

A couple edged back towards the trees.

"*Cinq—six—*"

The leader opened his mouth to argue, but his words were drowned by Romanetti's deep voice chanting:

"*Sept—huit—*"

There was a general scamper and crashing of shrub.

"*Neuf—dix!*"

There was no one in sight but for the Americans and ourselves.

Romanetti smiled contentedly.

"Spada," he said, "see that those rats do not return." Then, raising his hat to the Americans, "I must ask your pardon for the treatment you have suffered. They were not members of my own band or they would never have dared touch you. I shall see that such a thing never happens again."

By now the Americans were thoroughly enjoying their adventure.

"And what is your name?" the man asked.

Romanetti drew himself up. He was proud of himself and the position he held.

"I am Romanetti," he said.

"Romanetti!" the girl cried. "But how thrilling! Don't you remember, Father, they were telling us about him at the hotel?"

The man nodded.

"Yes, I remember, the ' King of the Brigands.

"'The King of the Maquis' is the title that I prefer,' said Romanetti. "And may I ask your name?"

"Why, yes. I'm Mr. Cass Mombley of Chicago, U.S.A. And this is my daughter, Geraldine. It's been a real thrill being kidnapped like that. But it might have turned out very differently if it hadn't been for you."

He asked Romanetti a lot of questions about the island and our mode of life. Finally, Romanetti insisted on providing an escort to guide them safely back to Ajaccio.

Evidently Mr. Mombley and his daughter were very grateful to Romanetti for the way in which he had come to their help, for some time later a very excellent silver-mounted rifle arrived. It bore the name of a celebrated gunsmith in Paris. Accompanying it was a note asking Romanetti to accept it as a token of gratitude for his chivalrous conduct to the Americans.

XI

Knowing Romanetti's character, many men have wondered how it was that he became an outlaw. He had more good points and a greater sense of honor than most "civilized" men. He was kindly and chivalrous, and once he had given his word nothing would make him break it. Besides all this he was innately moral. Naturally he had no jurisdiction over his men when they visited the village cafés and dance halls; and, men being men, there were women in the lives of most of our band. However, their amorous exploits had to be confined to their periodical visits to civilization. No women were ever allowed in his camp.

Much of his attitude towards women may have been prompted by his happy marriage—for Romanetti was married, and very happily, too. But his wife never came to his camp. He always maintained that the rough, chancy life we led in the mountains was not suited to women. Romanetti's wife and her small son lived in a little villa on the outskirts of Coggia, overlooking the sea. Periodically Romanetti would visit her, when his guides had reported that it was safe to do so.

Every bandit chief of any standing had a number of these guides, whose chief duty was the guarding of their leader's safety. They worked in with the bandits' spies in the various districts, collected the news and acted as spies themselves. When Romanetti, myself, Caviglioli, Bartoli, and any of the lesser bandit chiefs wished to visit a more or less civilized portion of the island, a number of these guides was sent out to report whether the coast [was] clear. Another of their duties was to precede their chief, when entering or leaving a house, so that they received the first shots from any ambush that the police might have managed to arrange in spite of the outlaws' spies and guards.

This drawing of the police fire upon themselves may sound a dangerous and thankless task, but the guides were well paid and were picked especially for their loyalty and devotion to their leader. Besides which, so effective was the system of intelligence employed by the outlaws, that it was very rarely that a guide received a salvo intended for his chief. It was just a matter of precaution.

Naturally the guides had to be men we could trust implicitly. A treacherous guide had it in his power to do a great deal of damage, thus only the most trusted men had this duty allotted to them. Besides which, they all knew the reward of treachery — certain death.

I had never met Romanetti's wife although I was anxious to, so, when one day Romanetti announced his intention of visiting the villa at Coggia and asked me to accompany him, I was very glad to accept. Life in the Maquis can be very monotonous, and I was feeling in need of a change of scene.

Guides were sent out to report on the advisability of the venture, and a messenger was sent to the villa to warn Madame Romanetti to expect us the following night.

Duly the guides returned and reported that the coast was clear. Romanetti at once set about his preparations. Various members of the band were detailed off to protect the villa, our horses were ordered round, and we set about clothing ourselves as befitted the occasion.

Romanetti was always most particular in his dress, and it has been said of me that I was the Beau Brummell[6] of the bandits. I

---

[6] A reference to George Bryan "Beau" Brummell (1778 – 1840), a celebrated dandy and friend of the Prince Regent and future King George IV. Brummell eventually fell out of favor and was forced to seek exile in France. During Britain's Regency era he was celebrated for his trend-setting, fashionable dress and piquant witticisms. When Brummell was snubbed by the Prince Regent at a private masquerade ball, he turned to Lord Alvanley and, referring to the masked Prince, asked: "Alvanley, who's your fat friend?" In the decades following his expatriation to France, numerous collections of Brummellian anecdotes and aphorisms appeared in print, many of them

certainly took a pride in my appearance. Though not over tall I was a well-built man, turning the scale in the neighborhood of thirteen stone, and I carried my clothing well. My silk shirts and my velvet jacket and trousers, so I have been told, were famous throughout the island, and were always mentioned by Corsicans to tourists when speaking of me. I wore, also, a gaily colored waistcoat with either silver or gilt buttons, a colored band round my hat and a bright silk tie. My belt and revolver-holsters were elaborately tooled. *Ma fé!* In those days I was a figure to set any woman's heart beating.

It was dark when we reached the villa and Madame Romanetti had everything in preparation for our supper. Romanetti adored her, and had lavished gifts upon her so that the villa would have vied with one of the rich businessmen's in Ajaccio or Bastia.

There was a spotless white cloth upon the table and gleaming silver and glass. We even had table napkins, and of this I was glad, for, by tucking mine into my collar, I was able to protect my silk shirt.

And the food, *dio mio!* I had not tasted a woman-cooked meal for very many months. Chicken and gravy and golden-brown potatoes and wine.

With very pleasant feelings of anticipation we sat down, after laying our guns on the cloth beside us, where they would be handy in case of emergency. I remember that Madame Romanetti insisted that we should first wipe our weapons for fear that the oil on them might stain her cloth.

Besides his guides, Romanetti had two guards upon whom he relied—two large wolfhounds that invariably followed him wherever he went, and slept by his bed at night.

---

fictitious, including the series *Traité de la vie élégante* (1830), published by Honoré de Balzac.

We had scarcely begun our meal when one of the hounds, that had been lying contentedly on the rug before the fire, rose to its feet and crossed to the window, walking with stiff legs and bristling hackles. With a rumble in its throat the other beast joined it.

Madame Romanetti started up from her chair.

"What is it, Nonce?" she asked, a scared look in her eyes.

"*Je ne sais pas de tout. Peut-être c'est le police.* You had better turn out the lamp, my dear."

Madame Romanetti did as she was asked while Nonce and I seized our guns. The room was faintly lit by the flickering fire. By its light I could see Madame Romanetti standing tensely with one hand on the shoulders of a wolfhound as though seeking its protection. Romanetti was by the window, his head on one side, listening.

Suddenly there came the clatter of a man's feet in the hall and the door burst open. I had him covered instantly but it was only one of the guides.

"*Dio mio!* The police!" he panted. "*Vite!* You may yet have time."

Romanetti called his dogs to heel, and ordering his guide to lead the way, followed him. We crossed the hall, but as the guide opened the door into the garden a volley of shots rang out and he fell to his knees. Romanetti and I leaped back into the dining saloon. Behind us we could hear the sharp crack of the wounded guide's revolver as he replied to the fire of the police.

Madame Romanetti, seeing our escape by the front door was cut off, had opened the window. She cried softly to Romanetti and me to jump.

I went first. It was a fair drop to the flowerbed below, but I landed safely on my hands and knees. I had hardly scrambled to my feet when Romanetti thumped down at my side. He was a much older man than I and he fell more heavily. I could hear him cursing in the darkness.

"What is it?" I asked.

"My ankle. It is twisted. Here, Spada, lend me a hand."

He hobbled to his feet but found that he could not stand.

"*Diable!* Never mind, I shall have to crawl. It will be safer, too, though slower."

So we set off through the shrubbery towards the shore.

From the other side of the house there came an almost incessant rattle and crash of shots. Our outposts had opened fire on the police and were, we trusted, keeping them too busily occupied to bother about us.

Romanetti, however, was not the only man to employ dogs. The police also kept a number of wolfhounds, or police dogs as they are called in Germany. They found them of great use in the dense thickets of the Maquis, or on night raids such as this.

One of these dogs, coming round the house at that moment, sighted us and gave the alarm. A shot from Romanetti's gun silenced it, but not before one of the police, evidently the one in charge of the brute, had sighted us and opened fire.

Dropping flat on my stomach in the undergrowth, I fired back at him, and had the satisfaction of seeing him crumple up.

Crawling and hopping, Romanetti eventually managed to reach the shore. Here we had a remarkable piece of good luck. Two fishermen, who had been about to set out on a night expedition, had delayed launching their boat when hearing firing from the direction of the villa. They immediately recognized Romanetti and very willingly helped him into their craft.

Unfortunately, however, we had not gone far from the shore when half a dozen police appeared at the water's edge.

"*Holà*, there, you in the boat. Come back! We wish to search you."

The two fishermen looked doubtfully across at Romanetti and continued on their way. A carbine cracked and something "plopped" into the water a couple of feet away.

Romanetti leant forward.

"It is no use, my friend. Turn back. We can swim for it. But row slowly."

The men nodded and swung the boat back to shore.

"Hold hard there," one shouted. "Can't you see we are coming."

One after the other Romanetti and I slipped over the stern into the sea. Using underarm strokes to avoid splashing we gently paddled out to sea. Then, once we were satisfied that it would be utterly impossible for the police to see us from the beach, we turned and made our way parallel to the coast until we began to tire. And it was not long before we did, clothed as we were and shod in heavy boots. At length, when we were almost exhausted, we turned in towards the land and crawled ashore.

For a long while we lay on the sand too weary to move. But a life in the Maquis toughens a man wonderfully, and presently we were able to start off on the return journey to our mountain camp.

Fortunately we were not far from the house of a small farmer who was in Romanetti's pay. There we were able to obtain the loan of a couple of horses. They were poor animals but better than nothing, especially as Romanetti's ankle was troublesome.

Towards dawn we crawled into camp, almost as much dead as alive. How different we must have looked from the two gaily dressed outlaws who had left camp the previous evening.

Most of our men had already returned, and later in the day our horses found their way back.

After a rubdown, a change of clothing and a meal, we lay down to sleep. It is one of the blessings of the healthy, open-air lives in the mountains we lived, that when we awoke we felt little the worse for our adventure.

That evening Romanetti called a meeting and totaled up the casualties. Honors certainly went to the bandits. We had lost two men; but of the police, so far as we could ascertain from our men, five had been killed and at least seven were known to have been wounded. Naturally it was difficult to gauge the enemy casualties in the semidarkness, but that the figures were substantially correct was later confirmed by our guides, who collected news from Ajaccio.

An expensive price to pay for a spoiled dinner with your wife. I often wondered whether Romanetti thought it had been worth it.

XII

The more I pondered over the surprise attack upon Romanetti's villa at Coggia, the more certain I felt that we had been betrayed by one of our own band.

Knowing, and trusting, our men as we did, it was difficult to credit this; in fact, when I talked the matter over with Romanetti, he resolutely refused to believe anything of the sort.

"You are doing my men an injustice, Spada," he told me. "We are all in this together and it is only by mutual trust that we can hope to withstand the authorities. All my men I have personally chosen and there is not one I wouldn't trust with my life."

"I know, but there are points about last night that can only be explained by believing that one of our guides had given us away to the police."

"What points?" demanded Romanetti, but I would not say. I could see that he placed such trust in his men that nothing I could say would alter his belief.

The greater part of the night I turned the matter over and over in my mind. The one question that I couldn't answer for myself was how the police had managed to approach so close to the house in spite of the wolfhounds with which we had supplemented our guard. The hounds in the house had given us a warning. How was it that those outside the house had failed to do so? And again, the police attacked the villa in a manner that indicated that they knew the disposition of our guards. How could they have known this unless one of our guides had betrayed us?

The following day I began an investigation upon my own account.

The two main questions I decided that must be first solved were: Why had the hounds given no warning? And, was there any man in our band who could have any reason for desiring the death of either Romanetti or myself?

Taking the first question, I set about finding out who had been responsible for the hounds on the night of the raid.

I was informed that a man named Castiglione had had the dogs in his charge that night. He was a tall, sullen-looking youth with a thatch of lank black hair that was continually getting into his eyes. He was not well liked by the others, but he had an almost uncanny power over the hounds, and for this reason was generally in charge of them.

Castiglione? There was something that I had once heard about him, but what? I sat in the doorway of my hut cleaning and oiling my carbine and trying to remember.

At last I had it. One of the guides had once told me that before Romanetti's marriage to his wife, Castiglione had been passionately in love with her. Naturally, he had had no chance against the great Romanetti. As a rival he had stood no chance.

Wasn't it possible that, ever since Romanetti had married the woman he loved, Castiglione had been obsessed with a longing for revenge? Wasn't it possible, also, that he felt, with Romanetti out of the way, he might have stood a chance of winning Madame Romanetti's favors?

I had found a plausible answer to both of my problems—a means of silencing the hounds and a motive for wishing to get rid of Romanetti.

The next thing to do was to see whether I could trace Castiglione's movements between the time the guides were sent out to prepare for Romanetti's visit to the villa and the night of the raid. I realized this would be a little difficult since Castiglione had been one of the guides detailed for this work and would therefore, naturally, have been absent from camp. On the other hand, the very fact that he had been one of the guides who had been entrusted with this work told against him, for he had both the knowledge of the proposed visit of Romanetti to his wife and the opportunity to get into touch with the police when, presumably, he had been making contact with some of our spies in Coggia.

There was the possibility, however, that he had been in the company of one of the other guides. This would definitely prove him innocent unless the other guide were also guilty of treachery.

I suppose I should have gone to Romanetti and put the result of my investigation to him before continuing with it. But, as he had been so definitely of the opinion on the previous day that the raid had been brought about by clever spy work on the part of the police and not by treachery in our own camp, I decided against the idea and continued with my inquiries alone.

Here I made a mistake. Rumors of my inquiries no doubt reached Castiglione, for the morning following he was missing from camp.

After this there was no need of further proof. He was self-confessed as a traitor.

Immediately upon the news of Castiglione's absence reaching me I went to Romanetti.

"I have found out the name of the man who betrayed us to the police," I told him.

He frowned at me.

"I thought I told you, Spada, that no man in this camp would betray me—even if he dared."

"There you are wrong," I retorted, "for Castiglione did."

"Castiglione? How do you know?"

I told him all I had discovered; how Castiglione had been a would-be lover of Madame Romanetti; how he had had the opportunity of getting into communication with the police, and of how he had been in charge of the hounds that night.

"It was easy for him to silence them," I told him. "Those hounds would have done anything for him."

"But this is all supposition," Romanetti objected. "You have no proof. Where is Castiglione? Bring him here."

"That I can't do," I replied. "He was here last night. This morning he is gone. He ran away in the night."

I have never seen a man in so terrible a temper; it was all the more fearsome because Romanetti was, by nature, a mild man.

"*Dio mio!* It is you who were right. I have been blind. Call all the men here." Then, when they were assembled in front of his door: "Go out, every one of you, and find Castiglione. There is a thousand francs for the man who brings him back alive—and a bullet for any man who kills him. I want that man brought back alive—do you understand? Alive!"

The Maquis is vast and possessed of a thousand safe hiding places, but we bandits were all used to its ways and we knew the most likely refuges that Castiglione would choose. However, it was almost a week later before he was brought back to camp, safely bound and slung across the back of a mule.

Romanetti strode up to the prisoner and stared fiercely into his terrified face.

"Cut him loose," he ordered, "and give him a gun."

One of the bandits objected to this, but Romanetti turned savagely upon him.

"*Fripon!* Do as I say. This is a matter between this man and me. Give him a gun and leave us. If I am killed he is to be released. Those are my orders. Do you all understand? It shall never be said of Romanetti that he murders men as they do down in Ajaccio."

I did not like the idea at all. For my part I would have liked to have seen Castiglione dangling from the end of a rope. Give a man a fighting chance by all means, but a traitor, no! Even a bullet is too good. Place him on a horse, a rope from a branch about his neck, then whip up the horse. That is what I would have done to Castiglione; but Romanetti was our chief and if he wished to risk his life at the hands of a miserable traitor it would not have been healthy for us to interfere, much as we might have liked to.

So Castiglione was given a gun and we all retired, leaving him and Romanetti in the clearing between the huts.

For a while they stood, talking. Then suddenly there came the sharp barking of a gun. From where I sat I saw Romanetti roll over in the dust and Castiglione, his lank forelock flapping across his forehead, leap across the yard to where Romanetti's horse was tethered.

He had only got halfway into the saddle when Romanetti's gun cracked out. Castiglione, with one foot in the stirrup, seemed to rise in the air before falling to the earth beneath the horse's excitedly plunging feet.

I ran up and was relieved to see Romanetti getting to his feet and dusting the earth from his clothing.

"You are not hurt?" I asked.

"Mais non," he replied calmly, "but if that devil hadn't been so nervous I would be dead. He shot at me when he thought I wasn't looking. However, he will never betray anyone again. Have him buried, though it is too good an end for him. He should be fed to his dogs."

Yes, Romanetti was a strange mixture of mildness and fierceness, with an odd code of honor of his own. What other man would have chosen such a way of settling with Castiglione? Most, with scarcely a trial, would have slung him by a rope to the nearest tree. Romanetti preferred putting a gun in his hand and giving him a chance of dying like a man, even though he had not lived like one. Melodramatic, perhaps, but what seems melodrama to the mind of a Northerner is commonplace and everyday to a Corsican, particularly to an outlaw.

XIII

Although outlawed from civilization, we still managed to enjoy a certain amount of its pleasures. There were cafés, inns and hotels where we were well known and where there was always a welcome for us. Our favorite of these was the Hôtel d'Orléans, near Vizzanova.

Possibly it appealed mainly to us on account of the ease with which we could reach it unobserved. It was easy to guard, too. Built on the mountainside as it was, with the Maquis coming to within a few yards of its back walls, we could arrive unobserved and, if necessary, leave at a moment's notice.

Our guides were sent to reconnoiter, and, if they reported all was clear, we would come down through the Maquis, entering the hotel from the back, spend a lively evening, eating, drinking and dancing, while pickets guarded the road on either side.

Though the Hôtel d'Orléans was our favorite, there were others we frequented. I remember one night Romanetti giving an especially lively party at one of these. Romanetti, though a strict moralist, was no prude, and a number of café girls had been imported from Ajaccio. There was an enormous amount of laughing and singing, and, as the pile of empty bottles accumulated, the café girls' voices grew shriller and shriller, so that the band had to play even louder to make itself heard.

It was in the midst of all this noise and confusion that the village priest walked in and asked for Romanetti.

At once Romanetti crossed the room to his side.

"*Je suis ici, mon Pére*. What can I do for you?"

To many it may seem strange that the village priests throughout Corsica looked upon us, not as the outcasts of civilization, but as members of their flocks.

The old man smiled kindly at Romanetti.

"I know, my son, that after your lonely life in the mountains it is good to come down here and make the night hideous with your caterwauling and screeching. But tonight there is a poor woman lying in the cottage next door. By the morning she will be dead; but you would not like her last few hours to be disturbed by your enjoyment."

"*Dio mio! No!*" cried Romanetti. Then, mounting the little stage that had been erected for the musicians, in a few short words he dismissed the company. Five minutes later the house was in silence.

Turning to the padre, Romanetti asked, "Will you take me to this poor woman? I would like to make my apologies."

I accompanied them. In a miserable little hovel next door to the inn was the sick woman. There was no doubt that what the priest said was true: she would not live to see a new day.

Romanetti fell on his knees by her bedside and asked her forgiveness for having disturbed her.

"For you see, *ma mère*, I did not know that there was anyone sick so close to *la taverne*, else we would have been more considerate."

She opened her eyes and recognized him.

"*Me fé! C'est* Romanetti."

Putting her withered old hand upon his head, she blessed him.

As he went out Romanetti called to a young man who stood by the doorway, and whom I took to be the old dame's grandson. I heard the rustle of some notes changing hands.

"You will need them," I heard Romanetti saying, "for the funeral."

There are few recreations in the Maquis and time is apt to hang very heavily on one's hands. We played cards, of course, and diced for money, but beyond that and our periodical visits to the fringes of civilization, we had little to amuse us. There was, however, hunting. This, besides being a sport, was a necessity. You cannot step round a corner of a street and ask a butcher to send you something for your dinner when you live in the Maquis. Your meals come either through the peasants and guides, who act as liaison officers with the outside world, or from your gun.

Romanetti was a keen hunter and a very expert shot. One morning he set out on horseback with his two wolfhounds and a man named Arna Goscapi as escort.

"Which way are you going?" I called after him, for I always liked to know where he could be found in case of emergency.

"Down the Valley of the Lava, then I can call on our sick friend."

"Our sick friend" was the priest of small village in the Lava Valley. He was extremely poor, and of late had been suffering from an affliction of the chest. Romanetti, in his usual kindly way, had taken him under his care. Only a few days before I had heard him giving instructions to Arna Goscapi to deliver some money at the priest's house to help him over his illness.

As I watched him ride off I little thought that it was the last time I should see Romanetti and that by nightfall I would be "King of the Maquis."

Late in the afternoon Goscapi came galloping back into camp. He was hatless and disheveled, and there was a wild, frightened look in his eyes.

He dismounted and ran up to my hut.

"Romanetti is dead," he cried. "The police—they ambushed us—we were riding down the Lava Valley when suddenly they shot from behind some bushes. They almost had me, too."

I felt stunned at the news. Romanetti dead! Of course we bandits always carried our lives in our hands; at any moment a shot might ring out and put an end to us. But Romanetti—he was so experienced a leader. It is the careless, the overdaring whom the police pick off.

"But where were the dogs?" I asked sharply. "They should have given warning of any ambush."

For a moment Goscapi hesitated.

"The dogs? Oh, they were off in the bush on the opposite side of the trail to the police. Romanetti had set them in after some game. And the wind was blowing from them to the police."

"Very well," I said. "Now tell all the others I wish to see them—at once."

In a few moments they were all collected in a semicircle about the door of my hut.

"Romanetti has been killed," I told them. "Goscapi saw him shot down by the police. You are now without a leader. Is it your wish that I, as Romanetti's lieutenant, shall lead you?"

What would they say? There were many amongst them who had served under Romanetti for a far longer time than I. Would they demand the leadership of the band? Ever since I had joined the banditti I had determined that one day I would be "King of the Maquis." Now that position was within my grasp. Would one of the others try to snatch the honor from me?

For a moment they were silent, looking from one to another as though deciding if there were a better man amongst themselves; then Pelosi, the eldest of the outlaws, cleared his throat and spat vehemently.

"Speaking for myself," he remarked, "I am satisfied. Though you have been a bandit for less time than most of us, you have proved yourself fit for the job of taking Romanetti's place."

There was a general murmur of agreement. Thus I found myself the leader of the most powerful band of outlaws in Corsica.

Two days later a peasant was brought in by one of the guides. He seemed nervous and asked to speak to me privately. I led him into Romanetti's hut, which I now occupied, and shut the door.

"Well?" I asked.

"I have something to tell you—can we be overheard? That man Goscapi, is he about?"

So he had something to tell me about Goscapi. The twinge of suspicion I had felt, when Goscapi hesitated before replying about the hounds, returned.

"What about Goscapi?"' I demanded. "Come on, man, spit it out."

"Well, I was working in my vineyard in the Lava Valley when I saw Romanetti riding down the trail. He had his two dogs with him and that man, Goscapi. The dogs were well ahead of them, working about in the undergrowth—one on each side of the trail."

"Yes—yes—but what about Goscapi?"

"I was coming to that. I saw it all quite clearly. Goscapi dropped back a little behind Romanetti—then quickly he fired—from behind. Romanetti rolled off his horse, and Goscapi, after making sure Romanetti was dead, galloped away."

First Castiglione and now Goscapi! And these were the men Romanetti had been ready to trust his life to. In that moment I determined that I would trust no man, however faithful he might seem.

"Go into that inside room," I told the man. "I will fetch Goscapi. Wait in there till I call for you."

Calling some of the men, I told them what I had heard from the peasant. The more hotheaded ones were for lynching Goscapi on the spot.

"No," I said, "he must have a fair trial. What do you say, Pelosi?"

Pelosi agreed with me.

"Bring him in, then," I commanded.

I think he must have realized at once that we knew, for there was the look of a cornered beast about him. But he tried to bluff it out. Possibly he thought we had no proof.

Then I produced the peasant.

Confronted by the man's story, Goscapi crumpled up and admitted that he had shot Romanetti from behind.

"But why?" I demanded.

"Because he was going to visit *Monsieur le Curé*."

Then I understood.

"That money Romanetti gave you for the padre, you kept it yourself?"

Goscapi nodded.

"*Si, si.* I have a girl in Ajaccio. I promised her money. I did not know where to get it, and then Romanetti gave me the money for *Monsieur le Curé*—so I used it for the girl. I was afraid when I knew that Romanetti was going to see *Monsieur le Curé*—so I killed him."

One of the men jumped up and started for the doorway.

"Where are you going?" I called.

"Why, to get a rope, of course."

"Not so fast," I said. "'Romanetti was the finest man I ever knew. He was my greatest friend. He would not have hanged this *crapaud*.[7] He gave Castiglione a fighting chance. I shall do the same. Which will you have, Goscapi, revolvers or knives?"

Goscapi chose guns, as he was an excellent revolver shot.

So we went out into the yard and Pelosi stood us back to back in the centre.

"Now," he said, "take fifteen paces each and then stop. When I cry 'Fire!' turn round and shoot. Understand?"

Goscapi nodded dumbly.

"Then start!"

I began counting as I walked, "One—two—three—four—five—six—seven—"

Suddenly Goscapi must have lost his nerve, for he let out a yell that was hardly human and began discharging his gun.

---

[7] Toad.

I threw myself flat on the ground and twisted round to face him.

He was running like a mad thing for the Maquis. Resting my gun on my left forearm, I fired. He turned a cartwheel like a shot rabbit and pitched forward into some bushes.

He was dead, but so was one of my men, and another wounded.

"Take him and bury him," I ordered. But they all refused. Finally one of them tied a rope to his feet and dragged him into the Maquis.

"We do not bury carrion," they said.

I had sent a messenger to the little white villa at Coggia to tell Madame Romanetti of her man's death. Some days later she and her small son, of about eight or nine years of age, arrived at our mountain camp.

"I cannot stay there alone any longer," she told me. "My place is in the Maquis where Nonce lived. One day his son will be a man and will take his place at the head of the banditti. He will be better fitted to do this if I bring him up in the Maquis."

So Romanetti's wife and son came to live in my old cabin and I undertook to have the lad trained in woodcraft and in the use of arms. He was a fine lad, even at that age, and showed much of his father's spirit and fearless determination.

One day, perhaps, the banditti may be a power in Corsica again; and if they are, young Romanetti will be at their head.

XIV

Romanetti had not only been chief of the most powerful band of outlaws in Corsica, he had also been the acknowledged "King of the Maquis," or, as the more poetically minded sometimes styled him, "King of the Green Palace."

I had now taken Romanetti's place at the head of his band and was therefore the most powerful of the bandit chiefs; but would I be acknowledged as "King of the Green Palace"? Neither Caviglioli nor Bartoli, the two most powerful bandits after Romanetti, had denied Romanetti's claim to this title. I felt, however, that there would be trouble before they were willing to recognize me in the same way. To them I must have been something of an upstart. I had literally shot my way into the forefront.

If I were to gain the distinction I had set my heart upon, I realized that I must make my power felt. The gifts to the peasantry must be kept up and, if possible, increased. To do this a regular and adequate income was an absolute necessity.

Some time previously, Romanetti had been granted the concession of carrying the mails between Ajaccio and Lopigna. From this we had derived an easy and substantial income. Then some interfering journalist from Paris had written about this practice in his paper and the concession had been withdrawn, and Romanetti had let the matter slide.

I had always determined that, if ever I succeeded Romanetti, one of my first acts would be an attempt to regain this contract. It was an opportunity both for establishing my power and swelling our revenue.

A week after Romanetti's death I sent a messenger to the *Commissaire du Poste* at Ajaccio reminding him that we had once carried the Ajaccio-Lopigna mails for a period of nine months, during which time no complaint of the service had been received. I demanded that the concession should be revived, and intimated that I was not prepared to take any refusal.

Rather to my surprise my demands were agreed to, the Postmaster stating that the rate of payment would be the same as previously paid. We also received the assurance that mail drivers and their escort would be exempt from any attempts at arrest whilst in execution of their duties.

Naturally I was delighted at this official acknowledgment of my power, and for the first few trips drove the mail myself with an escort of eight or nine of my men.

Rumors reached me that Caviglioli was enraged by my success. As the second most powerful outlaw in Corsica, he had hoped that upon Romanetti's death his own band would rule the Maquis. Now I had stepped into Romanetti's shoes and was receiving the allegiance of the peasantry formerly in Romanetti's pay. That before long there would be trouble between Caviglioli and myself I felt was certain; meanwhile I was determined to strengthen my position as much as possible.

For some months I retained the mails concession, then one day, without warning, when the usual driver and escort presented themselves outside Ajaccio to take over the mail coach, they were informed that their services would no longer be needed. Somebody had complained to the authorities in Paris and instructions had been received in Ajaccio that an official driver must be appointed. At once my men returned and reported to me that the concession had been withdrawn.

I may have been wrong, but in this I imagined I saw the hand of Caviglioli. I had learned that he was determined to oust me from my position and had said that although I claimed to be "King of the Maquis" he would never acknowledge me as such.

"And who is to drive the mail coach now?" I demanded, almost expecting to hear that Caviglioli had been appointed.

"Giovanni Ricci," I was told.

"Ricci? That *crapaud*? Never in this life," I retorted.

Romanetti had weakly knuckled under when his contract had been withdrawn. I was determined not to do the same.

"Here, Pietro," I called. "Go at once to the *Commissaire du Poste* at Ajaccio and tell him that I cannot agree to the withdrawal of our concession. If he does not remove Ricci I shall shoot him down and any other driver that they may replace him by."

The following day Pietro returned with his arm in an improvised sling. The *Commissaire du Poste* had angrily told him that he did not bargain with thieves and then, when Pietro was riding away, had shot at him, wounding him in the shoulder.

I at once set about making my preparations. The spot I chose for ambushing the mail coach was not far outside Lopigna. Here the trail ran through a rocky defile. The road was narrow and very soon my men had effectively blocked the way with large boulders. Then I settled down to wait, after having posted several guides on the hillside to watch for the approach of the mail coach.

Presently I received the signal that the coach had been sighted, and a few minutes later it rounded the bend, Ricci at the reins with a couple of gendarmes beside him, their carbines across their knees. I had expected that Ricci would be given an escort, so the presence of the gendarmes did not worry me; besides, I had chosen an excellent point to shoot from and had built up the boulders in such a way as to give me perfect protection.

At sight of my barricade Ricci drew in his horses, but I had planned my position well, for he was within range of my rifle as soon as he rounded the bend and was unable to turn back on account of the narrowness of the track.

Snuggling my carbine into my cheek I drew a bead on Ricci and fired. It was as clean a shot as I have ever made. Without a sound he pitched off the box. The horses reared up and one of the gendarmes was thrown into the road. The other I picked off with my carbine.

At the sound of my second shot the frightened animals bolted, and I had only just time to leap clear of my barricade before the mail coach piled itself upon it.

Meanwhile, the gendarme who had fallen from his seat had picked himself up and taken to his heels down the track towards Ajaccio.

"Let him go," I called to my men, "and come and cut these poor beasts free."

We released the horses and, when they had been calmed, we loaded the mail bags across their backs and upon our own horses and returned to camp.

Unfortunately, there was little of any value in the mails; we collected what little there was and burned the rest. We had, however, shown the Postmaster at Ajaccio that it did not pay to ride the high horse when dealing with André Spada and his band.

I did not know it then, but that day I had sown a seed that will come to flower upon the day the guillotine falls upon my neck—if ever that day comes.

XV

Under Romanetti's rule I had little opportunity of indulging in my one great failing—my weakness for pretty women. And since I had taken over the command of Romanetti's band I had far too much on my hands to trouble over much about love. But once I had firmly established my position and was satisfied that there was not a man or woman on the island who did not know that André Spada was the most powerful bandit in Corsica, I found my thoughts returning persistently to Marita, to Simone, to Maria and all the other girls I had known before I was exiled to the Maquis.

Of course there had been the girls of the cafés and dance halls, but they were different. They came to my hand as a strange horse would have come to a feed of oats. I was rich and I could give them pretty things to wear, expensive food to eat and wine to drink, and money to spend. But they were not the sort of women I yearned for: the edge was off them like a much-used knife. I like a clean, sharp blade fresh from the grinder's stone.

It was spring and the young oaks made an auburn haze in the Maquis and the mating birds filled the air with their songs and chattering. *Moi*, I felt restless and dissatisfied, unwilling to set myself to any definite task. I was in this mood when one of my men came to see me with news of a wedding in one of the villages bordering the Maquis.

"And the bride! You have never seen such a one. So beautiful that it is a sin to think of her marrying such a fat clod of a husband."

Here was an opportunity for a little mild enjoyment. I decided to make a surprise call at the inn where the wedding festivities were being held and see for myself whether this bride were as lovely as my man had described her. There is always an air of carefree jolliness about a wedding that leads to many a flirtation, if to nothing more; and I was in a mood for a little relaxation from the rather stern sort of life I was living in the mountains. So choosing half a dozen of the men who could be trusted to behave themselves in a more or less seemly fashion even though the wine might be flowing freely, I set off.

We arrived at the village shortly before midnight, and after taking the precaution of posting a man at both roads, I went in search of the inn. It was not difficult to find, for there were lights flooding out into the street from every window, and as I approached I could hear the place humming like a hive with the voices of the guests.

We found most of the party assembled in a long room at one end of the inn. The floor had been roughly polished and a few planks had been set on some casks at one end to make a temporary platform for the musicians.

I was dressed in my newest clothes, a velvet suit with gold buttons that had been specially made for me in Paris, and I was expecting to create something of a sensation. As it happened, I made even more of a sensation than I had reckoned on, for at my entrance the orchestra stopped playing and there was a general stampede for the doors. Some of the guests even attempted to climb out of the windows.

This was not what I had intended at all, so raising my voice to its loudest, so as to be heard over the confusion, I shouted:

"Wait! Everybody! There is no need for you to be frightened. I and my comrades are only making a friendly visit. We would like to dance and drink with you—and wish the bride 'Good luck.'"

They came back then, some rather doubtfully, and the musicians climbed up again on to their rickety platform.

Meanwhile, I had picked out the bride. She was as lovely—even lovelier—than my man had described. Unlike the majority of her guests, she had stood still, staring at me as though quite unafraid, when I had entered. Going up to her I said, "Madame, will you dance with me?" and, without waiting for her reply, I called an order over my shoulder to the musicians to play a waltz.

She danced beautifully, so I danced the next with her—and the next, and the next. In fact, I danced with her only, so that her fat lump of a husband scowled more angrily each time I took the floor with his pretty little bride; but he dared not say anything, for it was André Spada, the King of the Bandits, who had chosen to honor the bride with his attentions, and it was not healthy to argue with Spada. Who in Corsica did not know that? It was towards dawn that I wished her "Good-bye" and "Good luck" and left her, as I thought, to comfort her suet-faced husband.

On the way out I had a last drink with the innkeeper, who was a friend of mine and had more than once been of service to me.

As I reached the rail where our horses were tethered I was surprised to see that there was somebody seated on my mare. I was angry, too, for I allowed nobody to ride my mounts but myself. Striding up to my mare I roughly pulled aside the cloak that was covering the figure. *Sacré bleu!* it was the little bride who had given me so pleasant a night.

"*Ma petite!*" I cried. "What are you doing here? Where is your husband?"

At that she slid off the mare and threw her arms about my neck.

"Oh, Monsieur Spada, take me back to the mountains with you. I cannot bear to stay here now. The men of this village, they are but slugs. You are a man."

I was amazed, but at the same time there was no denying that I felt flattered.

"But, *chérie, votre mari*? What of him?"

"Oh, Jean. I do not love him. He is fat and old and ugly. It was only to please my parents that I married him. Take me to the mountains with you. Please, please take me."

What was I to do? I looked round at my men and caught sight of them sniggering behind their hands. What were they thinking? Were they whispering that Spada was afraid of the suet-faced husband?

Only that morning I had been cursing my fate because I had no woman to help relieve the tedium of my life in the mountains. Now a woman, and a beautiful one at that, had been almost thrust into my arms.

With a sudden laugh I swung myself up into the saddle and, stooping, lifted the little bride up in front of me.

"En avant!" I cried. "To hell with suet-faced husbands!"

And with a clatter we were off into the hills. On arrival at the camp I ordered another wedding party—a breakfast party this time—but with the same bride.

Two days later one of my men brought in the news that the bereaved bridegroom had shot himself.

I was a little sorry, for, looking at him, I would not have said that he had the guts to do it.

When I told her that she was a widow she was overcome with remorse and insisted upon my returning her to her parents' house. She seemed, somehow, to blame me for what had happened, though, seeing how she had begged me to take her, I cannot see how it was my fault. No doubt on returning to the village she spread stories of how I had kidnapped her after the dance and how she had fought for her honor. It was from women such as these that I got my reputation for kidnapping and, worse still, for rape. None of the stories that are told of my brutality to women are true, however, for few women came to my camp but of their own accord. True, there are times when I have stolen women, but it was from some other motive rather than a desire to possess them that I have done so.

More girls, and married women too, than I can remember have grown tired of the monotony of their own homes and run away to seek romance in the Maquis at the camp of André

Spada. It is their parents, seeking to whitewash their daughters' honor, who have circulated the stories of my kidnapping—the parents or the girls themselves, when they have tired of a mountain life and have returned to the villages; or I have tired of them.

There was one occasion when I kidnapped the wife of an official. There was an unfortunate ending to this adventure, an ending which never would have come about if the official had cared sufficiently for his wife's safety to have swallowed his pride.

It all began on a day when one of my favorite dogs strayed into the village of Bologna. A member of the municipal council, whose mouth was bigger than his brain, recognized the poor brute as mine, drew his gun and shot it. He had often boasted, so I learnt later, that there was nothing to fear about André Spada; that it only needed a man with a moderate amount of guts to put an end to my career. To bolster up this boast of his he had the dead dog carried out of the village and placed on the edge of the Maquis, where one of my men would be likely to come across it. To it he fastened a notice saying that he would do the same to me if ever I showed my nose inside Bologna.

It was not long before one of my guides discovered the hound and the note and brought both back to me. I was very angry because I had loved that dog. I say nothing against a man who shoots another in fair fight, but the man who will shoot a horse or a dog that is doing no harm is, to my mind, a low sort of worm. I determined that this official needed a lesson, not only for murdering my hound, but for daring to threaten me.

I sent out guides to find the man's house and discover which room he slept in, and, the night after having received the report, I picked four of my best men and rode into Bologna.

There was a balcony to this foolish official's bedroom, and for a man in perfect physical health it was as easy for me to reach his window as for a squirrel to crack a nut.

The window was closed, but with the butt of my revolver I smashed the glass and, slipping my hand through the hole, threw up the latch, then entered. A moment later I was standing at the foot of the scared official's bed, covering him with my gun while he sat up and gaped at me like a codfish on a fishmonger's slab. There was a lump under the bedclothes beside him which I guessed was his wife taking refuge at my sudden entry.

"*Maintenant*," I said softly. "Here I am, Monsieur. Why don't you shoot me like you promised you would? I am ready."

For a moment the man just stared, his eyes almost popping out of his face; then I saw his right hand creeping towards his pillow. So he slept with a gun under his head!

"*Tiens!*" I barked. "If you try any tricks I'll drill you full of holes!" and I advanced my gun threateningly towards his ponderous stomach.

At this, fearing for her husband's safety, the wife popped her head out from beneath the bedclothes and I was amazed to see how beautiful she was. It is an odd thing how these fat, ugly men can obtain young and pretty wives. This one had a mass of dark, curly hair and big soft eyes which were staring at me in a defiantly frightened way.

"Monsieur," she cried, "please do not hurt him. For my sake forgive him for shooting your dog. I will buy you the best in Corsica if only you will go away."

I removed my hat, and, placing it at the foot of the bed, bowed to her.

"*Mais non*, Madame. There are no better dogs in Corsica than I already have. I am sorry, but your husband will have to pay more dearly than by buying me a new hound."

It was at that moment that a fitting punishment occurred to me. I had valued my hound; no doubt this fat beast of an official valued his little wife.

"Madame," I said, "get up and dress. *Vite!*"

"Mais non, Monsieur, je vous prie—"

"Do as I say, please," I said firmly. "And you, Monsieur, if you move it will be the last thing you do in this world."

As soon as the official's little wife had dressed I backed to the window and whistled. Almost immediately one of my men joined us.

"Here, Pietro," I said. "Take this lady to the horses and wait for me there. If she screams gag her, but I do not think she will—she seems a wise little woman."

As soon as I was alone with the husband I ordered him, too, to get up. Standing him at the foot of the bed I lashed him firmly to one of the posts.

"And now, Monsieur," I said, "I shall leave you. You killed my hound and you insulted me. It is only right that you should pay for your little pleasures. The price I put on it is twenty thousand francs. I shall take it in one hundred franc notes. See that you have it ready when I call. If you inform the police or try any tricks you will never see your wife again. When you have handed over the money to me I shall see that Madame is returned as safe and well as she is now. I give my word of honor on that."

Madame was in tears when I reached the horses.

"Oh, Monsieur, what have you done to my husband?"

I reassured her and setting her before me I rode back to the mountains. On reaching camp I put her in the care of Madame Romanetti. Then I set about my preparations for the following night. I had already left two of my men behind with instructions to watch the man's movements and report if he attempted to communicate with the police during the day. Several of my guides were sent down to keep in touch with the two spies and meet me in the Maquis outside Bologna. Then I settled down to sleep, for if a man wishes to have all his wits about him he must both eat and sleep.

That night I met the guides as arranged, just outside Bologna, and received their report that the official had not communicated with the police and that there was no trace of any ambush in the vicinity of the house. It seemed that the man had decided to be sensible. No doubt his pretty little wife was very precious to him; certainly he would have had great difficulty in getting any other woman to look at him.

Swinging myself up on to the balcony outside his bedroom I tapped on the window. Immediately from within the room there came a flash and the report of a gun. The window shattered not six inches from my face and a bullet whistled away into the darkness behind me.

My own gun was in my hand, and without raising it I fired from my hip a stream of bullets breast high from one corner of the room to the other. Then, vaulting over the balcony rail, I dropped to the ground and ran for my horse, half expecting all the time to feel a bullet between my shoulder blades; but none came. I reached my horse in safety, and a few minutes later I was in the protection of the Maquis.

I was enraged at the man's treachery, not so much because he had tried to kill me — that was only natural — but because he had cared so little for his wife's safety that he had endangered it by his attack upon me. I returned to camp planning what revenge I could take to teach the man a lesson he would never forget. I even contemplated getting even with him through his wife. I need not have worried, for I had hardly finished my midday meal when one of my guides came in with the news that the official had been found dead in his bedroom. One of my shots fired at random had found a billet in his heart.

There was now no further revenge needed. The death of my hound and the insult to me had been wiped out. I went to arrange an escort to take the widow back to Bologna whilst Madame Romanetti broke the news.

It is strange what small incidents can lead to. My dog choosing to visit Bologna that morning cost the fat official his life, widowing a pretty little woman, and almost led to my own death. But, after all, life in the Maquis was like that to me; my way lay between death on one hand and a pretty woman on the other. I was as likely any day to receive a bullet as a kiss. The uncertainty added spice to life. I would never have made a successful shopkeeper: each day is too much like the last to them.

XVI

It was about the time that my parents moved from Lopigna to Coggia that I first met Mimi.

Mimi was not her real name, but it seemed to suit her, and after our first meeting I called her nothing else.

Things had been very quiet for some time. We had done nothing to stir the authorities into action against us, and, though Bartoli and Caviglioli rumbled threats against me like a pair of miniature Mount Etnas, they left me in peace. My receipts for protecting the merchants, hotelkeepers and the wealthier farmers were coming in satisfactorily, so that no action was required against them, or anyone else, to swell my revenue. In fact life had become deadly dull, and I was ripe for any mischief that might come my way, especially if it were a woman.

To relieve the monotony I and some of my men had gone down to one of the hotels to dance. There was the usual crowd of cheap girls there, and I was not expecting to get much of a kick out of the evening.

Presently I caught sight of a girl who had entered without my seeing her. She was dancing with Giocundi, the woodcutter. I was at once struck by her appearance. She carried herself proudly, her head thrown back and her gaze steady, almost fierce. She was such a contrast to the girls of the dancehall that I at once determined to dance with her.

The next time Giocundi passed where I was standing watching the dancers I stepped quickly out and, before he realized what was happening, I had relieved him of his partner.

Giocundi—the great oaf—only stuttered in surprise, and seeing who had taken the girl from his arms mumbled something and lounged out of the room, pretending that I was welcome to dance with the girl. If it had been anyone else but I he would have fought.

Then I looked down at the girl in my arms. She was gazing at me with a mocking smile on her lips.

" Well, *chérie*," I asked, " how do you like the change of partner? "

" Nobody could dance worse than Giocundi," she said.

We circled the room a couple of times before I spoke again. Then I asked:

"Well?"

"*Eh, bien!* You can dance a little."

"A little! *Dio mio!* I have been told that I dance better than any man in Corsica."

The girl threw back her head and laughed.

"You should not believe everything you are told, Monsieur."

Damn the girl and her impudence! If she were out to tantalize me she was going the right way about it. We danced a little more in silence. Then:

"You know who I am?" I asked.

"*Mais non.*"

"You do not wonder?"

"No. Why should I?"

"And your name, *ma petite*?"

"Why call me anything? We shall probably see nothing of each other after tonight."

Wouldn't we? I thought otherwise. Here was a girl with spirit; a girl whose eyes looked farther than a ten franc note and a bottle of cheap wine.

"*N'importe.* You need not tell me your name, my beauty. I shall call you Mimi. And as for never meeting after tonight— well, we shall see."

She looked sharply at me.

"*Hein?* So you too have a will? All right, *mon brave*, as you say, we shall see."

After our dance Giocundi came towards us as though to reclaim his partner, but I stared hard at him and scowled. After that he danced with one or two of the café girls and I forgot him.

I found a table for Mimi and ordered the best wine that they had at the hotel and the most expensive supper. If I had hoped to impress the girl I would have been disappointed, for she drank the wine with as blasé an air as if it had been water and took no more notice of the food than she would if it had been rolls and butter.

After supper she smoked one of my cigarettes, leaning her elbows on the table and breathing the smoke out slowly through her nostrils. She did not speak, just smoked and gazed at me with her eyes half closed as though she were looking at something behind my shoulder.

With a sudden movement she stubbed out her cigarette and rose to her feet.

"*Allons!*" she said. "Since you have frightened away my partner you had better dance with me."

After the dance I suggested that it was very hot in the room.

"Come out on to the verandah and let's get a breath of fresh air."

The verandah was at the back, and from it we could see the dark mass of the Maquis creeping down the mountainside almost to the orchard walls, behind it the vast bulk of Monte d'Oro craning its head up to the stars.

With a quick movement I seized the girl and swung her round to face me, saying:

"See here, Mimi, do you think you can treat me as you treat that lump Giocundi? You're the most tantalizing little devil I've met for years. Give me a kiss."

She threw back her head and gave a sound that was more like a snort than a laugh. I was reminded of my mare when she had one of her contrary moods: she would put her ears back and snort at me, and it would take a sharp canter with whip and spurs before the devil would be out of her.

"Me kiss you? Like hell I won't!" And out flashed her hand, catching me across the mouth with her knuckles.

Suddenly I was reminded of a song I heard an American sing one night when I was at the Hôtel Monte d'Oro:

> "I asked her for a kiss and, gee!
> Now what d'you think she said?
> She said she wouldn't kiss me
> So I kissed her instead!"

With a quick movement I jerked the girl towards me and began to kiss her fiercely, hungrily.

Fortunately I had my wits sufficiently about me to realize that her hand had dropped to my waist where I kept my knife. Releasing her sharply I seized her wrist. I was only just in time, for the point of the stiletto ripped through my silk shirt and drew blood just over my heart.

I bent her wrist till the stiletto clattered to the floor between us.

"You little hellcat!" I laughed.

Oddly enough I did not resent her attempt at murdering me. Instead I found that I wanted to take her with me to the mountains. Here was a girl with spirit who would make a good mate for a man like myself.

She would be able to hold her own amongst men and manage the girls—my so-called harem—better than any man could. She would be able to hunt and, if necessary, to fight.

In that moment as we stood glaring into one another's eyes, the light from a window gleaming on my stiletto on the ground between us, I knew that I must possess Mimi, even if I had to carry her off into the Maquis against her will.

I told her this in between my kisses, which she no longer resisted.

"And who are you?" she asked at length.

"*Moi?* Why, I am André Spada."

She pushed me away from her, but gently so that I released her when, if she had exerted her strength, I would have held her closer.

"André Spada. I should have known."

"Well, *chérie,*" I asked, "will you come or must I take you?"

Mimi crossed to the balustrade of the verandah and, leaning on it, stared up into the Maquis.

"*Mais oui,* André. I shall come. But first I must tell you my name. I am Marie Aimée Caviglioli."

Caviglioli!

"Luigi's sister?"

"Yes, Luigi's sister. Now do you still want me?"

What a strange twist of fate! That I, André Spada, the "King of the Green Palace," should have fallen for a sister of Caviglioli, the bandit chief of the "Ridge of Death"; a sister of the man who was out to kill me if there was no other way of depriving me of my claim to the kingship of the Maquis.

"Yes," I told her. "I do still want you. What difference does it make even if Luigi Caviglioli is your brother?"

She turned to face me so that a ray of light from the window lit up the fierce beauty of her.

"Very well then, I will come. But I warn you; you may find that you have not made a good bargain. I have a very strong will."

I took her roughly round the waist and, tilting back her head, looked into her dark eyes.

"And so have I, *ma petite,*" I told her. "*Sapristi!* But from down here they will see the sparks flying on Monte d'Oro."

I went to the doorway leading into the inn and beckoned one of my men.

"*Holà,* Pietro. Fetch my mare and a mount for Madame."

Pietro grinned, showing his broken and discolored teeth.

"*Si, si.*"

"But, André, what of my clothes? I can't come as I am."

And so Mimi was fond of her dress? All the better. I liked a woman who took a pride in her clothing.

"*Et pourquoi non, mon petit chou?* I have finer clothes at my camp than any I have seen in Ajaccio—frocks from Paris, furs from Vienna, jewelry from Rome. What more do you want?"

So Mimi mounted as she was, in her green and gold evening frock, and followed me to the mountains.

Ma fé! She was a tigress, that one. Beautiful and supple as a great cat, but her fangs and claws were barely covered. A word would be enough to set her growling and spitting.

Pietro from the first had shown himself interested in her. He would follow her with his eyes as she moved about the camp, his jaws working incessantly on the coarse shag he chewed.

Mimi had been with us about a week when a most fiendish din from the compound came to my ears as I sat writing in my hut. There were the shrill screams of an angry woman and the deeper, hoarser roaring of a man in pain.

Seizing my carbine I ran out into the yard. Then I stopped and, grounding my rifle, began to laugh.

Pietro, so one of the men told me, had taken a liberty with Mimi and now she was thrashing him with a yard-long horse whip.

Both the man's cheeks were scored from temple to chin by Mimi's claws, and already the blood from his back and arms was staining his shirt.

Several times he made a lunge at the woman in the hope of disarming her, but, in her left hand, Mimi held my stiletto, a prick with which was enough to make Pietro keep his distance. He tried also to escape from his tormentor, but he was a big, lumbering man shod in heavy knee boots, and Mimi had no difficulty in keeping up with him. In fact I imagined that she preferred him to run, as then he presented a better target for her whip.

Finally I had to intervene. If I had not, there is very little doubt but that Pietro would have been flogged to death. As it was, it was weeks before he was anything like fit for the saddle.

But the men had learnt their lesson and from then onwards Mimi was treated by them with the very greatest respect. It has been said that the female of the species is the most dangerous. Probably Pietro had never heard of this saying, but if he had he would most certainly have agreed warmly with it.

If Mimi had been content only to rule the men and girls at the fort it would have been peaceful enough. She evidently decided, however, that I, too, must come under her sway. This was entirely "another pair of shoes" and I was not submitting to her attempt.

Our quarrels became proverbial, and I have heard it said that when Mimi loosed her tongue upon me I groveled before her. This is not true. I have never groveled before anyone—man or woman. Certainly I gave in to her in many of her whims, and—ma fé—she had more whims than a dozen women. She was not content with the furnishing of her hut.

"So cold and bare!" she would cry, rolling her eyes in mock anguish.

"Then I will send into Ajaccio and get a mule train of furniture, chérie."

"Ajaccio! Ajaccio! Dio mio, André! There is no furniture good enough for me in Ajaccio. Send to Marseilles. If I am to be Queen of the Maquis, as you promised, I must have the finest and the best of everything. And you give me a poor stone hut and offer to send to Ajaccio for furnishings!"

So Marseilles it was. And not only tables and chairs and a divan, but rugs for the floor and hangings for the walls to hide their bareness.

Then when the winter came:

"Brr! André, these mountains of yours are cold. I must have bigger and thicker furs if I am to stay here with you."

Stay there with me? She was mine. She would not dare to leave me. I told her so, but she only laughed.

"*Chut!* André, you make my ribs ache."

But she was beautiful and her very waywardness attracted me more to her. A lover of horses, I like an animal with spirit: so with women. No milk and water wenches for me. Their place is in Ajaccio or Bastia.

I taught Mimi to shoot and gave her weapons for herself, a splendid little "Colt" and later, when the new rifle that I had specially made for me in Paris arrived, I gave her my old carbine. She wanted the new rifle, but upon that point I had my own way.

Soon she could shoot as well as any man in my band, myself excepted. She often came hunting with me, and her quickness of eye and the way she would set her horse at places that would have scared most men, won as much respect for her as her knife-edged tongue had.

But her vanity was appalling. She was never satisfied for long with what I gave her. The best in Ajaccio was only fit to wipe her feet on. I must send to France for almost everything for her. And her temper when resisted was devilish. Yet through it all I never lost my admiration for her, a certain proud tolerance that was fed, rather than damped, by her moods. Even, when in an especially fierce passion, she drew her gun and fired at me, I felt more of pride in her than anger.

It was lucky for me, though, that I was wearing my waistcoat of chain mail beneath my clothing, otherwise Mimi would have done her brother Luigi an unintentional service.

After that incident I tightened my rein upon her. I felt that she had had her head for too long;[8] she was getting the bit between her teeth and was likely to bolt, taking me with her.

---

[8] According to the Oxford English Dictionary, "having its head" is an equestrian idiom, used to describe a horse's behavior when it's unrestrained and is

There are some women whom it pays to be kind to: Marie Aimée Caviglioli was not one of these.

---

moving freely or running away. It implies that the animal is out of control, with no guidance from the rider. "When a horse has its head, it can pull away from the rider's control, making it difficult to direct or stop."

XVII

For a while my harsher treatment of Mimi seemed to subdue her. Her tempers were less frequent, and less fierce when they did come, and she seemed for the moment satisfied with her possessions, for she stopped pestering me for gifts.

But sometimes I would catch her watching me with the inscrutable look in her eyes of the cat tribe which she so strongly resembled.

When I was writing, reading or cleaning my gun in my hut, she would come in and sit in a corner, rest her chin on the back of her hand and gaze at me with her eyes half-closed.

At length this silent mood of hers began to make me uneasy. It was so foreign to her former tiger-like disposition.

She no longer accompanied me on my hunting expeditions and I missed her. I had got a lot of pleasure before in watching her eager speed in the Maquis and her animal-like skill as a huntress. Often my carbine had lain unused in its sling for a whole day's hunting while I watched Mimi making kill after kill. Now I hunted alone.

One day sport had been poor and I returned earlier than usual to camp. My mare was picking her way amongst the trees and shrub in the silent-footed way I had taken such pains to teach her.

A movement in a dense mass of undergrowth some distance away caught my eye. Thinking it might have been caused by a wild pig rooting around in the soil, I slipped from my mare's back and wormed my way quickly towards the spot.

Much experience of hunting and being hunted had taught me how to move through even the densest undergrowth as silently as a snake in spite of my thirteen stone. So it was that I came, unheard, to within ten feet of where Mimi lay in the arms of Giocundi.

So that was the meaning of her change of manner. So that was why she no longer came hunting with me. As soon as my back was turned she evidently slipped out of camp and met this damned woodcutter. Well, it would be the last time.

I could have shot them from where I lay, but it would not have satisfied my sense of justice. Besides which I was not so certain that I wished to kill Mimi. I was still passionately attached to her, and the blank in my life that her death would leave would be hard to fill.

Giocundi was another matter. I would kill him; but he must know whose bullet had put an end to his treachery.

There was a sapling behind where they lay. Snuggling my cheek into the stock of my carbine, I chose a spot on the sapling's stem just above their heads and fired. There came a scream, half of fear, half of anger, from Mimi and from Giocundi a mouthful of oaths.

They both leapt to their feet, Giocundi with his gun in his hand, and stared about them into the brushwood.

"Drop that gun," I snapped. "*Vite!*"

The gun glinted in the sun as it fell to the grass.

"Now your hands above your heads," I ordered, "and come out into the open."

Two pairs of hands crept up and I rose to my feet.

"Well, my beauties, so this is how you spend your time while I am away."

Mimi tried to pass it off.

"*Sacré bleu!* How you do take on, André. We were doing no harm. This is the first time I have met the man since I came to the camp."

The damned little liar! I knew her sort.

"*Hein?* So you were doing no harm." I raised my carbine. "Look at him for the last time, you little bitch, your precious lover won't be beautiful to see in a moment."

Regardless of my rifle, Mimi leapt forward, and throwing herself on her knees, clung to my gaiters, her fingers scrabbling against the laces.

"*Dieu en ciel!* You would not do that, André. You would not kill him. See, let him go and I will swear never to meet him again. I am your woman, André. If you kill him I shall kill myself, too. I swear it. Can't you believe me — trust me ..."

She burst into a passion of sobbing, beating her forehead against my boots and clawing up tufts of grass with her hands.

Without lowering my rifle I asked, "How am I to know that this will be the last time? Won't this rat come sneaking round here again as soon as my back is turned?"

She lifted up her face, ugly and furrowed by her weeping.

"Haven't I sworn it? What use will I be to you if you kill him? I shall hate you always — if I live. But if you spare him I will be faithful. Oh, can't you believe me?"

She was beating her fists against my thigh in her frenzy.

Well, I am weak with women. I gave way.

"*Eh bien*, I agree. But this slug shan't get off free."

I loosed my whip from my belt. And, dropping my carbine, took out my revolver with my left hand.

"Come here, you miserable firewood peddler. Nearer, blast you! Now how d'you like the taste of that — and that —"

My whip sang through the air and bit into the fellow's back and shoulders, coiling round him in a devilish caress.

He screamed in agony and made an attempt to rush me, but a shot from my gun whistling past his head held him back.

I kept up a position so that my back was never to Mimi. I did not trust her even after her wild protestation of faithfulness to me. She was the sort who would stab you in the back with as little compunction as a spider nips its victim into a living death.

So I thrashed Giocundi till the thong of my whip was dyed crimson, only ceasing when he stumbled unconscious into the undergrowth.

"And that's settled him, the bastard!" I said, kicking his limp body. "And as for you, my girl, catch hold of my stirrup strap. You shall run back to camp beside the mare while I ride. I'll take the edge off your pride."

And I didn't make the pace too slow, either, so that when we arrived in camp Mimi could barely support herself by my stirrup strap and her feet were torn and bleeding. It was only her pride that had held her up so long.

Later I went to see her as she lay moaning in her hut amongst all the finery she had made me get for her from Marseilles.

"Well,' I asked, "have I let the devil out of you?"

She only bit her lips and turned her face away from me.

"If ever you try that sort of game again," I warned her, "there is a bullet waiting for you. And if ever that slug-souled lover of yours comes nosing around here I'll shoot him at sight."

The next morning when I entered her hut Mimi was gone, and two of my horses.

I had been angry the day before, but it was nothing to the calm, fierce anger that burnt up in a cold flame when I realized that once again Mimi had tricked me.

The fools! Did they think Corsica—the whole world even— was big enough to hide them from my gun?

I called for my guides and instructed them to go out and find where Mimi and Giocundi were in hiding.

"Warn my spies in every village to keep a lookout,' I ordered. "But no one is to harm either of them. This is my vendetta and only my gun or my knife can satisfy it."

So perfect was my spy system that it was not long before I learned that the couple were in hiding at the house of some of Giocundi's relatives in Bastia, a town in the northeast corner of the island some fifty miles from my stronghold.

As soon as possible after receiving this information I set out alone for Bastia. Some of my most faithful men were very unwilling to let me go alone, but I would not have considered my vendetta accomplished if Giocundi and my late mistress met their death by any other hand than mine.

On nearing Bastia one of my spies met me and pointed out the house where Mimi and Giocundi had taken refuge. It was a square, flat-roofed building standing in a small garden on the outskirts of the town.

As soon as darkness fell I descended the mountainside, and, choosing a well-concealed spot in the shrubbery, I waited.

Either Giocundi had got wind of my coming or it was part of their plan to escape me by moving from house to house; at all events I waited all night without seeing a sign of them, and, as the light was creeping over the sea from the East, I was compelled to return to the mountains for fear of the gendarmerie. Giocundi had gained the first points in our game of hide-and-seek and a whole week had been wasted. Fuming with rage, I set out on my fifty-mile ride back to camp.

However, I was not accepting defeat: I had another plan which I felt certain would yield some results.

As soon as I reached camp I sent out a posse of men to the Caviglioli house with the instructions to bring back Mimi's young brother.

"Either we can find out from him where Mimi is in hiding or we can hold him as a hostage till the little hellcat is handed over to me," I said.

It was not long before young Caviglioli was standing before me. He was barely more than a boy, a slight, clean-limbed youth with a bearing and manner of speech so like his sister that at sight I hated him.

I had slept but little since Mimi's betrayal of me for that filthy woodcutter, and my nerves and temper were on edge.

"Where's your sister?" I demanded.

"I don't know," replied the lad, very quietly and calmly, "and if I did I wouldn't tell you."

I could have struck him across his sneering mouth for speaking to me like that—to me, André Spada!

How like Mimi he was! I sat and stared at him. Almost I could make myself believe that it was she who stood before me, answering for her desertion and ingratitude; the way he held his head, thrown back a little, his eyes half-closed, his lips slightly curled.

Suddenly he spoke.

"No wonder Marie Aimée hated you if you looked at her like that."

"What the devil do you mean?" I snapped. "And hold your tongue unless I speak to you. Now, for the last time—tell me, where is your sister? I don't believe that you do not know."

"You can believe what you like," he said slowly. "Anyway, I'm not speaking." And he closed his mouth just as I remembered Mimi snapped hers shut during our arguments.

One of my men, Carlo Farozza, an Italian, rapped the table with the butt of his stiletto to attract attention.

"Men can be made to talk," he suggested.

"What do you mean?"'

He laughed; his brown face puckered into a hundred creases.

"The Spaniards, they had a good old custom; what was it called? Ah, I remember—the Inquisition, *hein?*"

"You mean—torture?"

He shrugged his bony shoulders.

"Call it what you like, *mon ami*. If a man won't talk he must be persuaded to."

For a while I sat staring at the opposite wall, but seeing only Mimi—Mimi in Giocundi's arms.

Presently: "Take the prisoner away," I ordered, "and bring me something to drink—something strong."

For hours I sat there at the table, drinking and brooding. Wherever I looked I saw Mimi—Mimi in the dance hall that night in her green and gold frock, Mimi on the verandah with the light glinting on my stiletto on the floor between us, Mimi as she rode, as she shot, as she lay on her divan, as she groveled at my feet that last day in the woods—Mimi in Giocundi's arms.

Since she had left me I had scarcely slept at all, hardly eaten, living on my reserve energy and a consuming desire for revenge.

Neat whisky on an empty stomach is liable to go to even the strongest head. I think as I sat there drinking I can have been hardly sane; jealousy and neat whisky are to blame for what I did that night.

In the silence I seemed to hear Farozza's whisper in my ear—"Men can be made to talk."

And why not? How dared this unlicked cub defy me—and get away with it? He deserved anything that was coming to him.

"A man can be made to talk."

He *would* be made to talk! Spada was not the sort of man to be fooled by a youth. What would my men think if I allowed young Caviglioli to treat me with contempt?

As I crossed to the door I was surprised when I reeled and had to clutch the lintel for support.

It was very still out in the compound, still and cold. There was no moon, and the stars glittered like steel dust on a deep blue carpet.

An owl hooted. Then came the scream of a terrified rabbit as the jaws of some marauding fox cut through its soft fur. There are only two sorts of life in the Maquis—the hunter and the hunted. In the Green Palace Might is Right. It is a world ruled by the justice of power rather than the power of justice.

Sometimes I was the hunted; at others, the hunter. Now I was the latter and Mimi's young brother was my quarry.

"Farozza!" I shouted. "Farozza! Devil take the man. He might be dead, he sleeps so soundly. Farozza! Pietro!"

I had the youth led in and stood before me.

"This is your last chance," I told him. "Tell me where Mimi is and I shall let you go free. If not—"

But he just stood and stared at me as though I were some unclean reptile that had crawled into his house and that he would like to exterminate if he could do so without soiling his hands.

"So you have no use for your tongue?" I snarled at him. "Very well, if you have no need of it, it is an easy matter to relieve you of your tongue."

Of what followed I have no very clear recollection, and I am glad, for it is something I want to forget. The following morning the lad was found wandering on the outskirts of Ajaccio, blind in one eye and with his tongue cut out. I have said that I have only one regret, and that was for what happened to Mimi's young brother. And that is the truth. When I have killed, and that has been often, it has been in fair fight or to avenge some wrong. This youth had no chance of defending himself and he, personally, had done me no wrong.

There must have been some idea in my mind of striking Mimi through this youth. That she loved him I knew. Also I felt that when Mimi and Giocundi learned of what had happened to the lad they would suffer an agony of mental torture, for if I were prepared to punish an innocent youth so drastically, what might not they, the real offenders, expect once I had got them to my camp?

XVIII

My failure with young Caviglioli only made me madder than ever to be revenged upon Mimi and Giocundi. Nothing else mattered. Leaving the routine work of managing the gang, collecting our revenue, watching our security, to my chief lieutenant, Giuseppe Malaspina, I concentrated upon tracing the lovers.

The next intelligence I had of them was that they had been seen in Lopigna; so to Lopigna I went, although it was tempting Madame Guillotine.

It was evening and a cold wind was blowing down from the snow cap upon Monte d'Oro, so that I was not making myself in any way conspicuous when I turned up the collar of my coat and pulled my hat down over my eyes.

I had several men in my pay in Lopigna itself, so within half an hour of my entering the village at least half a dozen men were scouring the place for Giocundi, whilst I hid in the house of one of my friends.

Presently one of my spies came in with the news that Mimi and the woodcutter had been seen entering the cinema that evening.

Now, I felt, my quest was at an end. That night would be the last for the man who had stolen my woman and the woman who had deserted me.

I had my rifle with me, stowed under my cloak in two pieces for fear of exciting some inquisitive gendarme's suspicions. In half an hour's time the cinema show would be over. In that half-hour I had to find a vantage-point from which I could shoot as Mimi and Giocundi came out of the cinema, assemble my rifle and arrange a bolt-hole[9] for my escape. Cramming my hat

---

[9] Bolt-hole: a place of escape or refuge.

down over my eyes I hurried to the street in which the cinema was.

On the opposite side of the road to the cinema was a tobacconist's shop. The proprietor was just putting up the shutters. Living as I once had in Lopigna I knew him well—a bachelor, now dead, who lived all alone.

He was about to close the door when I inserted my knee into the jamb. He opened the door again to see who was there and I thrust my way in.

"Monsieur!" he cried rather testily. "*Que veut-toi?* It is late. The shop is closed."

I kicked the door shut behind me and locked it. Then, turning to him, I removed my hat so that he could see my face. He started back, his eyes flickering from me to the till upon his counter.

"Spada!" he cried. "What do you want here? I am a poor man. I am not worth your shot. I assure you I cannot afford to pay for protection. I am so poor I do not need—"

"Cut the cackle," I ordered. "I don't want your money. Is there anybody in this house but you?"

"No. I assure you I am all alone. Business is so bad a man cannot afford to marry, and I—"

Again I cut him short.

"Take me up to your front room overlooking the street. *Vite!* or I'll drill a hole in your skinny neck."

The man shuffled up the stairs in front of me and threw open the door of the front room.

"*Voila!* And now if you will excuse me I'll—"

"Come in and shut the door—and your mouth."

I crossed to the window. Yes, a perfect place from which to cover the cinema entrance. I wished that I had my Thompson gun with me, but the thing was far too big to carry about. My rifle would have to do. Quickly I took out the parts and began assembling them. In ten minutes the people would be leaving the cinema. I slipped a clip into the magazine.

"You have a back entrance?"

"*Oui*, Monsieur."

I lifted the lower sash of the window, and fetching a pillow from the bed tested the best positions for shooting down into the street.

"How d'you reach it?" I snapped.

"Down the stairs, Monsieur, and through the room at the back into the garden. There is a door at the end that opens into the next street. If you will allow me I shall go and see that it is open ready for your departure."

"You damned well *won't!*" I told him sharply. "Sit down in that corner there and keep your mouth shut."

A couple came out of the cinema, and another and another. I strained my eyes. Soon I would see Mimi and Giocundi, and then … Lovingly I stroked the band of my rifle.

Now the cinema was emptying in a steady stream. Soon now! But the stream was thinning. They must be coming out one of the last. All the better: I would have a clearer shot now that the crowd was dispersed.

Now the people were coming out in twos and threes again — the loiterers who had hung behind to avoid the crowd.

Sapristi![10] The man was closing the doors and the lights were being extinguished. I had missed my quarry again.

Though I knew that it was useless to wait longer I remained watching the cinema doors for another five minutes. At last with a curse I gave it up. Either Mimi and Giocundi had become tired of the show and left early or somebody had warned them of my presence in Lopigna and they had quitted the cinema by an emergency exit.

---

[10] An antiquated French curse word. A corruption of *sacristie*, used to indicate astonishment or impatience.

It seemed that the gods were fighting against me in my vendetta. But the more difficulties I met the greater became my desire to accomplish my revenge.

Warning the little tobacconist that, if he so much as breathed a hint of my having visited his shop, his house would be wrecked and his business banned, I went in search of my informant.

I found him in a little café in a back street, drinking absinthe.

"Well, *mon ami*," I said, sinking into a chair at his side, "either your information was incorrect or somebody has warned my birds."

He raised his brows inquiringly.

"They have flown? *C'est domage! N'importe*, I have found out where they are living—you can finish the job tonight after all."

It seemed that the wretched wood merchant had a wealthy uncle living in Lopigna, and it was at this man's house that he and Mimi had taken refuge.

My Lopigna *agent* led me to the house and, not wishing to get himself mixed up in any shooting, left me there.

Evidently Giocundi's uncle was well off, as my informant had suggested, for the house was large and possessed of a well-kept garden.

Choosing a clump of shrubbery that commanded a clear view of the house and entrance drive, I settled down to wait.

It was now close on midnight. If my quarry did not show up during the next hour or so I had decided to break into the house and rout them out. There was no need of this, however, for presently a light appeared in one of the ground floor windows. I craned forward eagerly.

There was a thin, light-colored curtain before the window, but I could see portions of the room through it. A moment later two figures came into view, a man and a woman, their forms clearly silhouetted against the curtain.

Tense with excitement I watched as they came together into one another's arms. How often I had pictured Mimi in

Giocundi's arms: now they were before me and I was letting precious seconds pass while I watched their passionate embrace.

Sighting my rifle I fired—once—twice. There was a crash of glass, a scream. 'The man had fallen while the woman still stood stupidly, as though stunned by what had happened. Again my rifle spat and the woman crumpled up and sank out of sight. My vendetta was accomplished.

Even as I stood up I heard voices and the slamming of doors in another part of the house. A hound had started to bay in the yard. I could hear the rattle of his chain as he fought to get loose.

There was no time to be wasted if I were to escape. Vaulting the low wall into the road I made at top speed for the Maquis. Although I met several men none of them attempted to stop me. I suppose they thought it was none of their business and they probably did not consider it would have been a healthy occupation to try stopping a running man with a rifle in his hand at that time of night. The natural presumption was that somebody had been killed and that, if any attempt were made to hinder me, some- body else would get killed. Besides which we Corsicans are far too used to the numerous shootings that result from vendettas to think of interfering. I understand that some of the larger cities of America are alike in this respect. If you happen to come upon a shooting you become at once deaf, dumb and blind, and remember an important appointment in another part of the town. In London, so I am told, the sound of a shot and the sight of a running man carrying a gun would be a signal for a wholesale manhunt. Plucky, perhaps, but to my mind unwarrantable interference.

There are few gendarmes about at midnight in a quiet little place like Lopigna, so it was that I gained the Maquis and mounted my horse without meeting with any trouble.

I was dog-tired when I reached camp and, my mission at last accomplished, I knew that once I laid my head on my pillow I would be asleep. I had had little rest since Mimi had deserted me and I needed some badly. But first I had to dispatch one of my guides to Lopigna to gather news, so that I might be assured that I had made a thorough job of my night's work.

I must have slept like a dead man, for when I awoke it was dark again and my guide had returned from Lopigna. I sent for him at once to receive his report.

Certainly the gods must have had a down on me[11] or else they loved Mimi, for in this vendetta of mine I had the devil's own luck. My guide informed me that the previous night my aim had been true enough and both the man and the woman had been found dead, the man with a bullet through the head and the woman with one in her heart. But—sacré bleu!—they were the wrong two. The lovers I had killed had not been Mimi and Giocundi, but Giocundi's uncle and the uncle's mistress.

And that was not all. There was another piece of news that was the talk in every café in Lopigna. The uncle had been wealthy: Giocundi was his heir. By my unfortunate mistake not only had I killed two blameless people, but I had rendered Giocundi a great service—I had made him a wealthy man.

But that was not the only news I received that night. A little later Pietro staggered into camp, his left arm hanging useless, a bloodstained rag wound about his upper arm.

While one of the girls was repairing his damaged arm I questioned Pietro.

"An ambush," he gabbled. "They got Giuseppe—shot him in the back as we rode past—they would have had me, too, if I had not lain along the side of my horse and rode like hell——"

---

[11] "To have a down on someone": to harbor a hostile or negative view. To bear a grudge or to intensely dislike someone, often unfairly.

"Who got Giuseppe?" I demanded. *"Les gendarmes?* Spit it out, you son of a bitch."

Pietro curled his lips back, showing his ugly, tobacco-stained teeth.

"Mais non. It was not the gendarmes. It was Luigi Caviglioli. Of that I am certain. I recognized one of his men."

Caviglioli! I could see trouble brewing. Warfare with the police was one thing: interbandit fighting was another.

I was not surprised, however, for Caviglioli had long been threatening my supremacy, and now this trouble about his sister had probably brought matters to a head. My determination to kill Mimi and her lover certainly gave Caviglioli an excellent excuse for starting trouble. Anyway, the prospect of a fight did not worry me. I was confident that I would beat Caviglioli with the utmost ease. My vendetta against Giocundi would have to wait. I was sorry for that, but if Caviglioli became really troublesome I would have my hands full enough without troubling about Mimi and the wood merchant. Anyway, a vendetta can wait: it is not a hot-blooded undertaking. Time would only add fuel to my hate and make the final reckoning all the sweeter. A vendetta may last a lifetime—and beyond, for one's relatives are always ready to accomplish what their dead kinsman has failed to carry out. "Clannishness" is almost a religion to the true Corsican.

As for Caviglioli I was glad that matters were coming to a head. While Romanetti had reigned over the Maquis both Caviglioli and Bartoli had been content to acknowledge his lordship, even to pay tribute to him when demanded. With Romanetti's death their attitude had changed. True they had kept their hands off any merchants or hotelkeepers who were enjoying my "protection," but they refused to acknowledge me as their overlord and looked with envious eyes upon the various profitable concessions and levies I controlled.

With the killing of my lieutenant, Giuseppe, and the wounding of Pietro, Caviglioli had declared open warfare. I accepted the challenge. Calling the whole of my band—except those on outpost duty—together in the compound I told them that any member of Caviglioli's band was to be shot at sight if he ventured into my territory. I also sent a message to this effect to Caviglioli and had all my spies warned to keep their eyes skinned.

Caviglioli's reply to my warning was typical of him. My messenger duly returned to camp, but lashed across the back of his horse—a dead man. Caviglioli had shot him and, knowing that the horse would find its way back to camp, had tied the body to the saddle and set it off on its return journey.

No doubt Caviglioli hoped that this fresh insult would lead to my making a punitive expedition into his territory and had prepared a hot welcome for me. If so he was disappointed, for I knew that if I waited long enough he would have to make the first move and I preferred to meet him on my own ground.

In this guess I was right, for even before I had expected him, he struck his next blow; and it was very nearly a fatal one for me.

Possibly I relied too much upon my guides and spies, for Caviglioli managed to penetrate well into my domain without an alarm being raised.

I was riding down the Lava Valley one evening with Pietro and a couple of my guides, when, without warning, there came a burst of firing from the Maquis some little distance away and my horse rolled over, pitching me into a clump of bushes. It was a very narrow squeak, for if I had fallen in the open, in less than a minute I would have had as many holes drilled in me as a honeycomb. As it was, I managed to squirm into the shelter of some boulders.

Pietro and my guides, seeing what had happened, had dismounted, slashed their horses' quarters and joined me behind the boulders.

For the next quarter of an hour we indulged in a sniping match with our attackers. It was impossible to tell whether they were police or rival bandits, but I had my suspicion that it was Caviglioli and some of his followers.

I was correct, for a little later I caught a glimpse of a red cap amongst the trees on our left. Caviglioli always wore a red cap, and I would have been willing to lay a bet that it was he. I could see his game; he was attempting to outflank us. But for my chance sight of Luigi's red cap he would have been able in a few minutes to enfilade us.

Motioning to the others to keep our enemies busy in front, I wriggled into a fresh position, from which I would be able to cover the spot from which I guessed Caviglioli had planned to rake our flank.

Either Caviglioli was careless or some of my old luck had returned, but presently I had a clear view of Caviglioli's head and shoulders as he peered out from behind a rock.

I snapped my sights on to him and let him have a clipful.

His head vanished from view and I could see the undergrowth swaying violently as though he were threshing about in agony on the ground behind the rock. A few minutes later the rifle firing petered out and I guessed that Caviglioli, if he were still alive, had called off the attack.

On the other hand, there was the possibility that one of my shots had finished Caviglioli, and his followers, finding that their leader was dead, had decided to make their getaway before things got too hot. After all, it was Caviglioli's picnic, not theirs, and if he were permanently out of the game there was little point in their carrying on. I hoped that this was the reason for this sudden retreat, but I wanted to be certain, so I instructed a couple of my guides to try and follow up my rivals' retreat whilst I scouted around.

Half expecting a renewal of the attack, I put my hat on the end of my rifle and poked it over the boulder behind which I was hiding. Nothing happened. Reassured, I ventured out into the open. Still no shot cracked out. It was pretty evident that Caviglioli's men had drawn off.

I investigated behind the rock where I had seen Caviglioli's red cap. There was quite a lot of blood about on the leaves and several largish chips of rock, one of which was deeply stained with blood. Clearly one of my bullets had chipped it off, throwing it into Caviglioli's face.

In the bushes from behind which Caviglioli's gang had been sniping us I found the dead bodies of two of his men. Fairly satisfied with my evening's work, I returned to camp to await my guides' report.

They did not return until well into the following afternoon, but the news they brought I found very satisfactory, for I had done Caviglioli almost as great an injury as if I had killed him.

Luigi was a handsome man and very proud of his appearance. Like many of us bandits he was a great lover, and the fascination that his looks had for the women of Corsica was almost as great as mine. *Mais j'avais changé tout cela.*[12] My shots had splintered some of the rock behind which he was hiding: one jagged splinter had smashed his jaw; another had blinded him in one eye.

But, though Caviglioli was my rival—and an unscrupulous one at that—I had no vendetta against him, and as the weeks went past and my spies brought in news of him, I began to feel sorry that one of my shots had not sent Caviglioli to his long final sleep.

---

[12] "But I had changed all that."

It was not that I feared his revenge; rather I was able to put myself in his position and feel a little of the desperate dread that must have been dragging at his heart. For my spies reported that, not only was his face permanently disfigured and his one eye totally destroyed, but that there were very grave fears of the blindness spreading to his other eye. Certain nerves had been injured and it was a toss up whether they would mend or snap.

Death, I knew, would be preferable to Caviglioli. Blindness would mean the relinquishing of his leadership. I doubted even if his followers would give him protection. More probably he would be turned adrift in the Maquis, where, if he survived, he might find asylum with some kindly peasant, though it was more probable the authorities would get hold of him and either death or lifelong imprisonment would be his fate.

Never to see the green beauties of our island again, never to look on a pretty woman or along the sights of his gun—for Caviglioli that would be a living death. Far better if one of my bullets had made a clean cut of his life instead of condemning him to—this!

But the gods must have relented, for his sight gradually improved and finally he died as he would have wished—killed swiftly by a bullet in open fight. But before that happened he was to hit back at life in a way that left its mark on the island.

XIX

I, as the rightful King of the Maquis, stood on my own and played my game as I thought best, except on those occasions when another of the bandit chiefs requested my help against the authorities.

Caviglioli, however, had an ally in Joseph Bartoli. Together they carried out many daring raids and, when my feud with Caviglioli became really serious, Bartoli was called in to help.

It is an excellent proof of the strength of my position that these two, set upon my extermination, were unable to accomplish it; though they certainly constituted a serious menace.

Bartoli was younger than Caviglioli, brave, intelligent and energetic. He had all the attributes of a successful leader and was exceedingly popular amongst his men and the peasantry.

One of his most daring feats was the burning of the Ajaccio Casino in 1930. This was a magnificent building that had only just been erected at a cost of about two million francs.

During its erection Bartoli had been in negotiation with the proprietor with regard to the proportion of the takings he was to receive for protection. Either Bartoli was taxing the undertaking at a higher figure than it would be likely to afford, or the promoters of the Casino did not believe that he would carry out his threat to burn the building if they did not agree to the percentage he demanded. Whatever the reason for the lack of agreement, the Casino was finished and Bartoli's demands had not been satisfied.

One thing that a successful bandit chief must remember is that he must never threaten unless he means to carry out his threat.

Bartoli had threatened to burn the Casino; so burn the Casino he had to unless he would be looked upon as a bluffer and subsequent demands would be treated with contempt.

No doubt the promoters of the Casino felt that Bartoli wouldn't dare to enter Ajaccio to carry out his threat. It is one thing for a bandit to carry out a raid on a village such as Lopigna or Coggia, and entirely another to risk appearing in Ajaccio itself.

Bartoli realized this and called upon Caviglioli to help him.

Between them they mustered a force of roughly a hundred and fifty fully armed and mounted men, and bringing with them a string of pack mules laden with inflammable material, they descended upon Ajaccio.

On the way to the Casino they made hay of the streets through which they passed, smashing windows and terrifying the inhabitants.

Arrived at the Casino, they set about firing it, and before long the building was burning away merrily.

Bartoli and Caviglioli had thrown out a cordon of their followers in the surrounding streets to ward off any police attacks and to turn back the fire engines that arrived like moths about a candle.

Adjacent to the Casino was the British Consulate, and at one time it looked extremely likely that it would become involved in the fire. The British Consul, seeing this danger, came out to reason with Bartoli, but was treated with little respect. In fact he was informed that if he did not return to his house and leave Bartoli in peace the Consulate would meet the same fate as the Casino.

All night the building burned; by the morning there was very little to show for two million francs and many months' labor.

Bartoli got nothing out of this escapade beyond a reputation for being a man of his word. However, I look upon this burning of the Ajaccio Casino as the foundation of the edifice of events, culminating in the affair of Guagno-les-Bains the following year, that led to the final break-up of the bandits' reign in Corsica.

One of the strictest rules of the Maquis was that foreign visitors were free from interference. It was a wise rule for at least three reasons.

To begin with, much of the prosperity of the island depended upon the rich tourists who visited it. If we bandits started molesting them, some, at any rate, would stop away, and the receipts of the hotels and shops would fall off. That would not have suited us at all, for a very large proportion of our income was derived from the hotels and shops in return for our "protection."

Then again, there were the authorities to be reckoned with; we could levy toll upon the prosperous islanders and, when necessary, enforce our levies by gun or fire without the police taking more than a mild interest in the affair. But shoot a foreign tourist, or even relieve him a little violently of his wallet, and there would be the devil to pay. Complaints would be received in Paris, and almost immediately pressure would be put upon the authorities in Ajaccio, and, whether they liked it or not, a punitive expedition would have to be dispatched.

A third reason for our standing off the tourists was the need to keep in with the peasantry. Not that we had anything to fear from them, but we found them such useful allies that we could not afford to offend them. They looked upon the tourists as the geese that laid the golden eggs. If we were to kill any of the geese and so cut off the supply of golden eggs the peasants would have been less inclined to act as our intelligence service, with the result that we would have had far more to fear from the occasional police expeditions against us.

In our levies upon the rich merchants, shopkeepers and hotel managers, we had the peasantry behind us. We presented these people to the peasants as tax dodgers who used their influence to keep down and "milk" the poorer class of the island. We thus, in the eyes of the peasantry, had a very high-minded reason for extracting every possible centime from the richer classes, especially as a proportion of the tribune received found its way into their pockets.

Though it was rather a matter of expediency for the outlaws to keep their hands out of the tourists' pockets, it did not prevent some of us from casting covetous eyes upon these obviously wealthy people who wandered unprotected and unmolested about the island.

During some of my occasional parleys with Caviglioli he told me that if only he could devise some scheme by which he could levy tribute upon the tourists without antagonizing the peasantry he would do so. As I pointed out, it would have to be some seemingly disinterested and high-minded excuse if it were to satisfy the poorer classes, and that at all costs no personal violence must be used as we would have a visit from the military, which was quite a different matter than the spasmodic police raids.

Personally, I was dead against the idea of attempting any interference with the tourists. I felt that it was bound to end in disaster. But Caviglioli was wedded to the idea, and nothing I could say would ever have altered his mind.

However, it was not until the summer of 1931 that he had a scheme for milking the foreigners without setting the peasants against him. Even then it was not his own scheme, but an idea suggested to him by his wife, Antoinette Leca.

She was a clever woman, was Antoinette Leca, and as beautiful and as true as she was clever. Briefly, her idea was this:

Guagno-les-Bains was the Lido of Corsica. The hotel proprietors and shopkeepers of this town had for some years past been doing all in their power to attract the wealthier tourists. One of the attractions they had devised was the provision of a swimming pool where visitors might swim and bask in the sun with very little more on than they wore when they first came into the world. In other words, it was permissible to bathe practically in the nude. News of this license soon spread, and those tourists who could afford the exorbitant charges of the hotels and shops and who cared for that sort of thing swarmed to Guagno-les-Bains like wasps to a jam pot.

Naturally, it didn't matter a twopenny cuss to us outlaws whether the tourists clothed themselves like the bathing belles of the nineteenth century or appeared as lightly dressed as Adam and Eve: we have never been accused of being puritanical. The artisan and peasant classes, however, viewed the matter far more seriously; and it was this fact that gave Antoinette Leca her idea.

Why not, she suggested, descend upon Guagno- les-Bains under the banner of public decency and heavily fine the sun-bathing tourists? What peasant was likely to object to so high-minded a motive? It was an excellent scheme and Caviglioli seized upon it hungrily.

His first move was to send a letter to each of the hotel proprietors of Guagno-les-Bains demanding that in future all their guests should be properly clothed. He knew perfectly well that the managers of the various hotels would not show the guests these letters. It was merely a move on his part to obtain public sympathy for what he intended to do. Incidentally, he saw to it that the news of these letters having been sent was widely distributed amongst the peasantry.

Naturally, no improvement in the matter of clothing was observed. Caviglioli was now ready for the second move in his game.

Garbing himself in his finest clothes and accompanied by a large number of his best men, all mounted, Caviglioli descended upon Guagno-les-Bains at a time when the greatest number of sunbathers might be expected to be there.

So it was that the tourists of Guagno-les-Bains were amazed, and possibly a little thrilled, to hear the thud of galloping horses and see a large band of heavily armed men bearing down on them.

Caviglioli had instructed his followers to round up the sunbathers, and presently several hundred of the tourists were herded together inside a circle of mounted bandits. Then Caviglioli addressed them.

He was a good actor, was Caviglioli, and a fair orator. For five minutes he treated them to a pious sermon on their "indecent exposure." He would not allow, he told them, the fair beauty of Corsica to be sullied by the sight of so many practically nude people. He wound up by saying that they each would be fined five hundred francs, an equivalent of about five pounds or twenty-five dollars.

Naturally, Caviglioli expected a refusal to pay this fine, so he was careful to inform them during his harangue that any man or woman who refused to pay would be carried off to the mountains clothed, or rather unclothed, just as they were.

None of the bathers had as much as five hundred francs with them, so while some remained on the beach as hostages, others were dispatched to the hotels to collect the fine money.

Caviglioli would, no doubt, have liked to make the fines a thousand or more francs a head, for the tourists could easily have paid it, but he was afraid that if he demanded too much the visitors might decide to wear more clothing or even leave the island. That would not have suited him, as he was determined to "milk" the place systematically.

Presently the emissaries returned from the various hotels with supplies of money, and all the fines were paid—all but two. A couple of young American girls announced that they were not going to be "blackmailed" in this fashion and resolutely refused to pay their fines. I don't for a moment suppose that this refusal to pay was prompted by anything other than a desire to see whether Caviglioli would carry out his threat and take them with him to the mountains.

No doubt Caviglioli never expected any of the visitors to refuse to be fined. However, the girls had called his bluff and he was faced with the choice of either losing prestige or taking the girls with him. After a moment's thought he decided on the latter course, and the two girls, clothed as they were, were swung up in front of a couple of the bandits and whisked away to Caviglioli's camp, the "Ridge of Death" as it was called, on account of the number of police who had lost their lives in attempting to storm it.

The two young American girls, no doubt, got an enormous kick out of their adventure, and were no worse for it when, two days later, they were returned to Guagno-les-Bains. I have little doubt but that Caviglioli treated them well—too well, so it was rumored, for the report got round that their visit would have been more prolonged but for Antoinette Leca's becoming jealous of them and demanding their return to Guagno.

Not unnaturally, the tourists were seriously annoyed at Caviglioli's raid, and fearing a repetition, they informed the hotel proprietors that either adequate protection must be provided or they would leave the island en masse. This placed the hotels in an awkward position, for they were mortally afraid of giving offence to any of the bandit chiefs, yet they dared not run the risk of losing their visitors. Finally a police expedition was sent out to capture Caviglioli.

My spies were the first to learn of this punitive expedition, and I at once sent a runner to the Ridge of Death to warn Caviglioli.

It may seem strange that at one moment Caviglioli and I are out for one another's blood and the next I am warning him against an attack that, if it had been successful, would have rid me of my rival. It was a rule of the Maquis, though, that in times of danger from the authorities all interbandit feuds were forgotten and a common front was exhibited to the police.

As was only to be expected, the expedition proved to be little more than a farce, and the police had scarcely returned when a message was received from Caviglioli reminding the tourists that he proposed to pay another visit in the near future and enforce further fines if there were no improvement in the "morals" of the Guagno-les-Bains bathers.

The police having failed them, the chief businessmen and the proprietors of the three big hotels at Guagno held a meeting. At this meeting it was decided that the only thing to do was to appeal to me for protection. Consequently, the following day I received a request to come to Guagno-les-Bains, my immunity from arrest being guaranteed.

I went and was met by a dozen very worried-looking men. Their spokesman begged me to provide protection for the tourists for the rest of the season, promising immunity from police interference for the guard I provided.

"For see, Monsieur Spada," he explained, "if that rogue Caviglioli again offends our visitors we shall be ruined—they will all leave the island and none will return next season."

"That is so," I agreed, "and what do you propose paying me for this protection?"

"Fifty thousand francs," suggested one.

"One hundred thousand," I replied firmly.

Evidently they had agreed upon the amount to which they would go, for my counter offer was accepted with such alacrity that I felt sorry I had not asked for more.

"That is, of course, for protection for this season only," I pointed out. "If you wish for protection next season the charge will be two hundred thousand francs."

I saw a look of consternation in the faces of these prosperous businessmen. Two hundred thousand francs! It would be like pulling their teeth out without an anesthetic.

"*Mais pourquoi, Monsieur?*"

"Well, this season is half finished. Next year, no doubt, you will require protection for the whole season."

They nodded glumly.

"But, Monsieur Spada, we would not willingly put you to so much trouble. Would it not be possible for so powerful a man as you to kill this man Caviglioli—*le fripon*—or at least put him out of action so that there will be no further fear of his annoying our visitors?"

I considered the suggestion, then:

"*Mais oui,*' I agreed, "it would be possible—at a price."

"And the price, Monsieur?"

"A quarter of a million francs."

Then followed a heated debate, the businessmen offering only a further one hundred thousand for this service, but fearing I might withdraw my offer of protection, they finally agreed that if Caviglioli were satisfactorily disposed of, I was to receive a further two hundred thousand francs.

As soon as our negotiations were complete I left for the mountains to arrange for the protection of Guagno-les-Bains. But news travels quickly in the Maquis when a bandit chief may be expected to pay well for it. Thus before I had reached my camp Caviglioli knew that my help had been requested and was preparing for his new stroke.

It fell swiftly, for the following evening he rode into Guagno-les-Bains with at least a hundred of his men behind him. He must have very fiercely resented the appeal to me for protection, for he rode through the town shooting the glass out of the windows and lamps and smashing everything that could easily be broken.

The inhabitants were terrified, and retreating inside their houses, remained there till the last bandit had left the town.

But Caviglioli was not troubling about them beyond smashing their windows to let off his feelings. The hotel proprietors and big shopkeepers were his quarry.

He began by surrounding the chief hotels and forbidding anybody to show their nose outside the doors. Then he informed the managers that they each would be fined the sum of fifty thousand francs for daring to seek my help against him. The shopkeepers were told to find a further fifty thousand, for, so Caviglioli said, if they could afford to pay two hundred thousand francs for his death they could afford to pay that sum to atone for their impudence in seeking my protection.

Probably nothing serious would have come of this raid if a German visitor had not very foolishly stuck his head out of a window at one of the hotels. One of Caviglioli's men, fearing the German was about to shoot, dropped him with his carbine.

This killing of a German tourist was a most unfortunate occurrence for all us bandits; in particular for Caviglioli. The French Government could not be expected to overlook this incident, and by the action of one of his men Caviglioli had lost the support of some of his most useful allies — the peasantry.

Both Bartoli and I condemned the killing of this tourist, for we knew what it would mean. However, true to the law of the Maquis, we stuck to Caviglioli during the ensuing trouble; but, deserted by the peasants, Caviglioli was the first of the great bandit chiefs to fall.

But for the killing of that German, he and Bartoli might still be alive and I be in possession of my liberty.

That one bullet had more far-reaching results than any other that had ever been fired in our stormy history. Who could have guessed, when Caviglioli's follower pressed his trigger, what it would lead to? *Mais, c'est la vie.* Some of the smallest seeds grow into the biggest trees.

XX

Without claiming to be more farsighted than either Caviglioli or Bartoli, I realized that after the affair at Guagno-les-Bains things had gone too far.

When Romanetti had ruled over the Maquis such acts of violence had rarely occurred. True, the island had felt the weight of his hand, but provided his levies were paid regularly, he did not raise that hand in terrorism. Caviglioli and Bartoli, acknowledging his power, had been content to follow his example.

With Romanetti's death and my accession to the leadership of the Romanetti band, Caviglioli and Bartoli had begun to appear in their true colors. They refused to acknowledge my right to control them, and had begun a reign of violence that culminated in the death of the German at Guagno-les-Bains.

Though not possessing Romanetti's gentle spirit, I had tried to enforce my demands peaceably, resorting to force only when I was opposed. To the leaders of my rival bands violence was as the food they ate and the air they breathed. We represented two rival points of view. I believed that our purposes could be better served by peaceful "protection"; they held that a reign of terror would produce the best results.

Naturally, a certain amount of threats and punishments were needed, or the various big business interests would have begun to think that they were paying for a protection that was no longer necessary. But Caviglioli, and in a lesser degree Bartoli, overdid their aggression, and as a consequence brought about their own extinction.

Realizing that Corsicans are not Frenchmen, the French had always ruled Corsica with a lenient hand, leaving the inhabitants to settle their disputes in their own fashion so long as they did not overstep the mark and embroil foreigners in their quarrels. They realized, for instance, that the vendetta was an institution they could not hope to stamp out. It was something in the blood of the Corsican that no amount of policing of the island could eradicate.

Probably of all nationalities the Corsican is the truest to his family. To us the bond of family is, and always has been, almost a religion. The word "brother" is looked upon as the highest term of endearment. A wife even, if feeling particularly attached to her husband, will call him "brother." It is from this attachment—fanatic attachment a Northerner would no doubt consider it—that the vendetta has arisen. A man kills your brother; you do not appeal to the authorities. We Corsicans would despise a man who did not personally revenge his brother's death.

Most of our native songs are of the vendetta. They are taught to us as children, and we are born and reared to the knowledge that a man, if he is a man, will avenge a wrong done to another of his family. And it is not only a matter of "an eye for an eye, and a tooth for a tooth." There is a line in one of our Corsican songs that very aptly phrases our sentiments. It goes something like this—"Though twelve men should die it would not even avenge the dead man's—boots!" You have it there, in a word, the sentiment that inspires the vendetta.

When one realizes that historians have placed the number of men killed each year through the vendetta at anything between two hundred and nine hundred, it is easily understood the problem that faces France in her administration of Corsica. Evidently the authorities early came to the decision that we should be allowed to kill each other as freely as we wished so long as we concentrated upon killing one another and left the foreigners alone.

In the burning of the Ajaccio Casino and the affair at Guagno-les-Bains the limit set by the authorities was overstepped, with the result that one day in November of 1931 two troopships, with an escort of destroyers, arrived at Ajaccio, and a war that was to last over eighteen months was put in train.

The transports brought a force of six hundred police and military under the leadership of men from the *Sûreté de Paris*.[13] I had been warned of the impending arrival of this expedition, and I had my spies waiting in Ajaccio to obtain all the details possible.

From the news that my spies brought back to me I realized that we were up against the most determined effort yet put out to exterminate the banditti.

Pietro was one of the men I had sent to collect information. He came back, his eyes rolling, his jaws working incessantly on a large plug of black tobacco.

"Dio mio!" he cried. "It is the end. They have brought armored cars and small tanks such as I have seen used in the War. With my own eyes I have seen them. And the machine guns! *Sapristi!* It is indeed the beginning of the end. Only today three airplanes arrived."

I tried to laugh his fears aside.

"What can they do?" I asked. "They are but Frenchmen. They do not know the Maquis as we do. We shall snipe them as they attack, and when they return our fire we shall not be there."

Pietro spat out his wad of chewed tobacco and cut himself another piece.

---

[13] Sûreté de Paris: a French police division, founded in 1812, that specialized in criminal investigations and public security. One of the first organized-crime investigative units in the world, it later became part of the Sûreté Nationale. Like Scotland Yard, the Sûreté focused on urban crime and detective work. And like the FBI, it dealt with national cases in coordination with other agencies. In the early 1930s, the Sûreté focused on organized crime and political unrest. Utilizing forensic science and surveillance, it coordinated efforts with regional police to apprehend fugitives and dismantle criminal networks.

"But no," he replied, "it is as I say—the beginning of the end. They are recruiting as many men as know the Maquis. There is one, Vazi, a young gendarme of Nice who is well acquainted with the mountains. He is to lead one of the attacking forces."

Vazi! The name was familiar.

"Do you mean Luigi Vazi?" I asked. "He who used to live in Bologna?"

"*Si, si.*" Pietro nodded violently. "He is a son of one of Caviglioli's women. It was a sad day for Caviglioli when his own son joined the accursed police."

It was disturbing news that Pietro had brought. Not only were the latest arms and equipment to be used against us by the largest force that had ever been sent to dispose of us, but the services of men well used to the Maquis were being sought. Vazi, I knew, would be of very great use to the authorities, and if rumor were true, some of the smaller bandits were being granted immunity if they would consent to guide the police and military through the Maquis.

On the same day I received messengers from Caviglioli and Bartoli asking for my cooperation. Though the expedition was mainly against these two I realized that while the authorities were there in strength they would not be content with rounding up my rivals; my own extermination would follow as a matter of course. Besides which I was bound by agreement to assist either of the other two in emergencies such as this. I therefore sent replies that I would be glad to cooperate, and asked them to attend a meeting at my fortress so that we might fix on the best methods of meeting this invasion.

At this meeting all personal animosity was forgotten. Fortunately, perhaps, I had still failed to trace Mimi and Giocundi, or otherwise cooperation between Caviglioli and myself would have been impossible. It was rumored that, with the money left him by his uncle whom I had killed, Giocundi had left Corsica, taking Mimi with him. This is quite possible, for if they had remained on the island my spies would have discovered them before this.

My plan for meeting the situation was that we should entrench ourselves in the mountains and let the police and soldiers expend their energy in trying to dislodge us.

Caviglioli and Bartoli, hotheaded as ever, were for meeting attack by attack.

"For see," Caviglioli said, "if we allow them to obtain a firm foothold in the Maquis they will freeze us out. Both Bartoli and I agree that we must show them that we are not afraid of them."

"That is all very well, *mon brave*," I said, "but you underestimate their strength and determination."

Caviglioli only laughed.

"Have they ever succeeded in beating us on our own ground yet?" he asked. "The Maquis is ours: no French swine are capable of routing us out of it. I am not worrying, Spada. Why should you? Why, today I go to Bologna. It will take more than a few Frenchmen to pen me up in the mountains."

"To Bologna? To see your woman there?"

"*Si, si!*""

Then I asked him a question that shook him out of his complacence for a moment.

"You know," I said, "' that the son of your woman at Bologna—Luigi Vazi—is leading one of the posses against us?"

He didn't know.

"*Diable!* Is that so? *Dio mio!* That a son of mine should turn traitor!"

After that we could get very little sense out of him, he was so upset, and presently he left for Bologna.

I watched him ride away. In many ways he was a fine man, even if he were my rival. He was quite fearless, and though to a Northerner's way of thinking a cruel and dangerous man, he was true to his code. He rode down the mountainside away from my camp, his scarred mouth set grimly, his one eye gleaming expectantly. I never saw him again. In life I had hated him as a rival, in death I admired him. *Ave* Luigi! Perhaps one day somewhere else we may meet again.

One can understand the bitter hurt that the news of Luigi Vazi's presence in Corsica as a member of the expedition against us was to Caviglioli. One only needs to remember the sacredness of their relationship as father and son to realize what Caviglioli felt. Here was young Vazi, the son of a favorite mistress of his, a child who bore his father's name, turning his hand against his own father when, by the age-old code of our island, he should have been standing shoulder to shoulder with those of his own blood in defiance of a common enemy.

Caviglioli was always foolhardy. He should never have insisted upon carrying out his visit to Bologna now that the foreign force had landed at Ajaccio. True, he was counting on their not yet being prepared to attack, but he was trusting too much to the friendliness of the peasants who no longer looked upon him as a friend after the Guagno-les-Bains episode. To them it was an unforgivable thing to have shot a tourist—a man who came to the island to spend money. A bandit who shot a tourist was no longer worthy of their protection. So thought the peasants, and one of them, seeing Caviglioli arrive at Bologna, jumped on his horse and rode as fast as he could to Ajaccio to sell the news.

The news was received gladly in Ajaccio. Though the expedition was not yet ready to start this seemed too good an opportunity to miss, so at once a number of gendarmes were dispatched to Bologna. The cars intended for the use of the expeditionary force had not yet been unshipped, so a number of private vehicles were commandeered. The one containing Vazi was the first to reach the inn where Caviglioli's mistress lived.

So quick and unexpected was the attack that Caviglioli's guides had been unable to give warning in time for him to make his escape. In fact, the guides had barely burst into the room where Caviglioli was with the cry: *"Les gendarmes! Vite! Allez!"* when Vazi's car skidded into the inn yard and the gendarmes leapt out, their guns drawn.

Though taken by surprise Caviglioli was always prepared for an attack. The gendarmes never reached the inn door, for no sooner had they left the car than there came the rattle of gunfire. Two gendarmes were killed instantly and Vazi received a bullet through his left arm.

Vazi, seeing that it would be madness to try to rush the inn, retreated behind the car and kept up a revolver duel with Caviglioli and his men without realizing that he was shooting it out with his own father.

It was not long before a couple more carloads of police and soldiers arrived, and Caviglioli, realizing that he was outnumbered, decided to make his getaway before it was too late.

Leaving a couple of his guides to draw the police fire to the front of the inn, Caviglioli and the rest of his men slipped out through a back window and made for the Maquis.

But Vazi had been expecting this move, and on the arrival of the rest of the police, had slipped out from behind his car and taken up a fresh position where he could see the back of the inn.

No sooner had he got into position than three or four bandits appeared from the rear of the house and made for the Maquis at top speed.

Vazi was an excellent shot, and although the men were a fair distance off and moving fast, he managed to pick one of them off with his rifle. The rest of the men succeeded in reaching the Maquis and safety.

Vazi ran up to make certain his man was dead. The bandit was lying on his face in the short grass, his arms flung forward, his rifle still gripped in one hand. Vazi, turning the dead man over on his back, found himself looking down into the face of his father.

There must have been a great conflict of emotion in the young gendarme's heart at that moment. He had succeeded in doing something that any of his companions would have given a year's pay to accomplish—he had killed one of the three great bandit leaders of Corsica within the first few days of the expedition's arrival. But it was his own father who lay dead at his feet.

He didn't have long to sort his feelings out, for suddenly there came a wild scream from the inn and a woman ran out.

To add to Vazi's confusion he recognized her as his mother—Caviglioli's mistress.

For a moment she looked down at the dead man, then, with a fierce cry, she snatched a gun from Caviglioli's holster and fired at her son. But Vazi was already well known for his quickness of mind, and although half stunned by the shock of having killed his father, he was too quick for the woman.

With a swift movement he knocked her arm up and the bullet whined away into the Maquis.

She would have fired again, but with a jerk of his wrist he neatly disarmed her.

Though young Vazi may have had little love for his mother it must have been a relief when a couple more gendarmes ran up and relieved him of the cursing and screaming woman.

In recognition of his having disposed of Caviglioli, Vazi was put in charge of the force that was sent out to round up the rest of his father's band.

His knowledge of the Maquis, gained in his early youth, was invaluable to Vazi, and within a week he succeeded in carrying out a coup that brought him fresh honor in the eyes of the authorities, although it made his name stink in the Maquis.

It was Bartoli who brought me news of this fresh victory for Vazi.

He appeared at my camp looking very tired; his youthful features seemed many years older since Caviglioli's death.

"*Sacré bleu*, Spada!" he began. "That son of a pig has the devil's own luck. Only yesterday he made a raid on that deep cleft on the west slopes of Monte d'Oro—you know the one. We have always thought it one of the safest retreats. But Vazi knew of that cliff path leading into the top end and sent a posse there whilst he blocked the bottom end. There were about a dozen of Luigi's men there and he blew them out into the open with hand grenades and then shot them down like a lot of rabbits. Two of them were his cousins. But what did he care? *Rien!* That man is no Corsican: he is only fit to be a Genoese."

To be called a Genoese is probably the worst insult a Corsican can devise. To turn on your kith and kin is the worst crime a Corsican can commit. Therefore Bartoli called Vazi a Genoese.

"He has gone too far, that Vazi," he said. "If I do not kill him with my own hand you may say *rimbecco* to me and the shame will be mine."

Rimbecco is the reproach that rests on a man who fails to avenge the death of someone dear to him. In former days the expression was looked upon as such an incitement to bloodshed that the word was banned, and any man heard using it was either banished from the island or had his tongue slit.

I tried to reason with Bartoli.

"What is the use?" I urged. "They will only have you, too. Wait till they attack and then you may have your revenge. Vazi knows the Maquis too well for you to hunt him out. Remain in the mountains and when he hunts you then will be the time to strike at him. Besides, what was Caviglioli to you?"

Bartoli polished the lenses of his field glasses before replying, then he said very quietly, "He was my own brother"; which, though it was not genealogically correct, was sufficient answer for me.

I wished him luck and he rode out of my camp down the mountainside into the Maquis, as Caviglioli had done less than a week before.

The sun was setting stormily in a November sky, striking the Maquis with its dull red rays so that the trees took on the appearance of a sea of blood. I felt within me, as the crimson flood swallowed horse and rider, that I would never see Bartoli again. Possibly it is our Southern blood; possibly our lonely life in the Maquis, but there are times when, hardheaded men though we are, we grow fanciful—superstitious if you will. In that moment I knew that Bartoli was doomed.

For the next ten days I had reports from my guides as to the movements of both Bartoli and Vazi.

Through sticking to my original plan of keeping to the mountains I still had a number of guides ranging the bush. The peasants, though they had turned against Caviglioli, yet stood solidly for me, and I could count upon them to give my guides faithful reports of the enemies' movements, and at the same time supply Vazi and his force with false details of my movements.

For ten days there was a constant guerrilla warfare between Bartoli and Vazi, but from my reports I could tell that Vazi was getting the better of it. Bartoli's followers were dwindling till only about a dozen remained. Some had been killed, others had deserted, some even had surrendered.

The end came one day when Bartoli found himself cornered and surrounded in the neighborhood of Coggia, where Romanetti's wife had once lived.

Vazi gave Bartoli the chance of surrendering, but he might just as well have saved his breath.

Bartoli must have seen that the end had come, but he determined to fight it out as long as he lived and his ammunition held out. No doubt he hoped, too, that even if he were killed, Vazi might share the same fate.

Vazi's luck held—the man with the charmed life, they had begun to call him—and he survived the fight unhurt, though for three hours there was almost incessant firing.

At last a lucky shot from Vazi's rifle found a billet in Bartoli's brain. With their leader's death, Bartoli's men surrendered. Vazi had added yet another sprig to the laurels he was gaining in his warfare against the banditti.

XXI

Now there remained only myself of the three great bandit leaders of the Maquis. If I had made the same mistakes as Bartoli and Caviglioli had done—antagonizing the peasantry and underestimating the powers of the police—I, too, would probably have been dead.

The death of my two rivals left me the undisputed King of the Maquis and in many ways strengthened my position. A large number of the followers of Caviglioli and Bartoli turned up at my camp and were duly enrolled in my band. I had now a larger following than any other bandit had ever possessed, and with the peasantry solidly favoring me I felt fairly secure.

However, I was determined that I was not going to make the same mistakes as my dead rivals. I would leave the attacking to the police and military and content myself with strengthening my position in the mountains.

My first move was to remove my headquarters to Caviglioli's stronghold, the Ridge of Death, as I considered it a better position to defend than my own fort. For one thing, it was more strongly built; besides which it was situated on a high ridge of ground commanding an uninterrupted view of the surrounding country. It was almost impregnable; if only Caviglioli had been content to stay there Vazi would never have succeeded in getting him, provided that he had not been starved out or run short of ammunition.

When I arrived to take over the Ridge of Death I was met by Caviglioli's woman, Antoinette Leca. In the excitement of the previous few days I had forgotten about her strangely enough, for I had always been immensely attracted by her. Looking back I wonder that, on the death of Caviglioli, her welfare had not been my first thought.

Remembering how it was a bullet from my rifle that had scarred Luigi's face so terribly, and deprived him of one eye, I was a little doubtful as to how Antoinette Leca would receive me. I need not have worried. She was immensely pleased to see me, and, forgetting my old feud with Luigi, looked upon me only as his ally who had been willing to come to his aid in a time of danger.

Yes, I had always admired Antoinette Leca; but before I had been many days in my new quarters I realized that I loved her. And she? Well, she learned to love me, too. She has remained faithful to me through all my difficulties and trials: even now, caged as I am in Ajaccio Prison, I have the consolation that she still cares, that nothing, even death, can really separate us. .

One would think that a woman in an outlaw's camp would be more hindrance than help; but with Antoinette Leca this was not so. She could shoot as straight and as quickly as any man I have ever known, and she was an excellent horsewoman.

Antoinette wore trousers, scorning the use of the skirt as unsuitable for our mountain life. In her cap, with a bandolier about her and guns in her holsters she looked every inch a man—and I have known no man I would sooner have by my side in a tight corner.

As I had foreseen, we were not greatly troubled by direct attack. The military made a few attempts at my new fort, but we had no difficulty in warding them off.

Supplies were our chief concern. Milk, butter and meat we had in plenty, for we kept a herd of goats for the supply of the first two necessities, and for the meat we had the abundant game of the Maquis and the wild sheep of the mountains—the *mufro*.[14] But there were other things we needed: bread, wine, ammunition, and it was of these that the authorities hoped to starve us.

---

[14] Muvra or mouflon (*Ovis aries musimon*): a feral subspecies of primitive domestic sheep, emblematic of Corsica.

It was not long before I arranged a system of "dog trains." We always had a large number of highly trained dogs in our camps, and on occasion previously we had used them for carrying messages. Now I decided to try them as smugglers of necessities from the outer world to our camp. The experiment was successful.

The dogs at once seemed to know what was expected of them. We would fasten a note to their collars and they would slip through the police cordon to some of our friends—and they were many—and bring back the goods we required in pouches fastened on either side of them.

After a while the police got wise to this scheme, but even then the dogs managed to slip through. We lost very few of them.

There were times, of course, when it was necessary to get through with bigger loads than the dogs could carry. Then a number of the men would shoot their way through the police lines, collect the goods at a prearranged spot, and shoot their way back into camp again. It was always possible to choose a spot where the cordon was weakest, as my spy system was functioning as well as ever. It was possible that the peasants were grateful for all I had done for them in the past and were glad to show their gratitude by being of assistance at a time when I needed their help most. They had also probably come to look upon me as a settled source of income. No bandits, no pay for spying! So, if only for this reason, there was an inducement to help me in my fight against the police. Besides which, I was still paying them for their services in spite of no longer being able to collect my levies from the townsfolk. During my nine years of life as a bandit I had collected quite an appreciable amount of money and valuables, added to which was the store that I found in Caviglioli's camp.

The cold of the Corsican mountains has to be experienced before its severity can be realized. Even in the summer the snow lies on the heights of Monte d'Oro, Cinto, Rotondo, Padro and others. In the middle of winter the cold is fierce, even for men used to it as we were. For the police, though they were lower than we and had the shelter of the bush, it must have been almost unbearable. I was not surprised, therefore, to feel the vigilance of the watchers slackening, and receive reports from our outside men that the majority of the expedition was being withdrawn.

Possibly, the withdrawal of a large portion of the police and soldiers may have made me careless; anyway, whatever the reason, a little later I had one of the narrowest escapes of my life.

I was riding along a narrow mountain path connecting Ajaccio and Palneca. I had with me only one of my guides and about four of my dogs. As they had been taught to do, these dogs were scouring the roadside some hundred yards ahead of us. Presently, one of them started barking in the tone that meant "danger," not "game"—one learnt to recognize their various sounds. At the same moment there came the spluttering clatter of a machine gun.

I could guess pretty well what had happened. The dogs had come upon an ambush of police machine gunners and one of the police, startled by the dog's sudden appearance, had let off a burst of firing. I could picture the wrath of the officer or sergeant in charge of the squad against the man who had unwittingly warned me of the ambush.

Whirling our horses round we set them off hard on the road we had just come by; but escape wasn't going to be easy for us that day. The road wound round the hillside, the cliffs towering above us on one side and dropping away to the valley on the other. A couple of miles away we saw, to our consternation, a police car travelling fast in our direction. Evidently it contained a fresh squad of police coming to relieve the one into which we had so nearly run.

It was a nasty position for us. Both above and below the cliffs were too steep to climb except with great caution. If we attempted to escape this way we would be at the mercy of the police rifles. If we turned back we would run into the machine-gun squad. If we went on we would meet the police car.

But I had not spent nine years being hunted in the Maquis without getting to know the woods and the mountains as well as the average man gets to know his own back garden. I knew that within fifty yards of where we were was a cave about fifty feet below the level of the road. If we could reach that we would be safe.

At this point the hillside fell sheer to the valley below. To climb down was impossible: however, I always carried a rope slung to my saddle. Unwinding this, I dropped one end over the cliff face and fastened the other to a projecting rock.

Ordering my guide to slide down the rope I unslung my rifle. At that moment the police car swung round the bend into view. I let off a burst of firing and had the pleasure of seeing the car lurch violently and narrowly escape going over the edge. I had hoped that by firing at the tires I might succeed in precipitating the police into the valley. If the driver had not been exceptionally skillful I would have succeeded.

There came a shout from my guide below to let me know that he had safely reached the cave. Giving the police car a couple more rounds that shattered the windscreen and made the occupants duck behind the dashboard, I slipped over the edge and a moment later joined my guide in the cave.

I had barely reached safety when the rope coiled past us and fell to the rocks three hundred feet below. The police had cut it hoping that I would be dashed to death.

Finding that I had disappointed them the police started a futile stream of bullets, hoping for a ricochet. They might have saved themselves the trouble. They even tried rolling boulders over the cliff, though how they imagined one could hit us I cannot think. How long they kept this up I don't know, for we did not wait to see. The cave ran into the hillside, and following an underground water- course—then dry—we came into a ravine about half a mile higher up the mountain. From there it was easy to work our way back to camp without being seen.

There were two things that happened the next September that are worth recording. The one affected me very deeply and I never really recovered from it; the other, though it did not really interest me personally, gives an insight into the workings of the vendetta.

This latter incident concerned Dominique Ettori, who, with Rutili and I ten years previously, had carried out a raid upon the house of a man named Sena. I had been looking for the traitor Marchi who had sold me to the police when I was in hiding in Barcelona, and had traced him to Sena's house. Ettori, who evidently had a score to pay off against Sena, had taken the opportunity of shooting down his enemy. I remember the occasion well, and Ettori's subsequent regret that he had not shot the widow and her two sons, Jean and Francois, also. He had feared the vendetta.

He was subsequently arrested and tried for the murder of Sena, and although I used my influence with the various witnesses so that he obtained his acquittal, he left the island and had not been heard of since. Then one day, ten years after he had vanished, one of my spies brought me details of his death.

It seems that immediately upon his acquittal Ettori had left Corsica and gone to live at Nice.

Sena's two sons had been brought up by the widow with the one great aim in their lives of avenging their father's death.

Jean Sena was now twenty-eight. Since the age of eighteen he had gone about with a loaded gun in his hip pocket, living for the day when he should meet Ettori.

Then, quite by chance, he was drinking at a café in Nice, when a man came in. Jean Sena did not take any particular notice of him until he heard the man ask the proprietor:

"Are there any letters for me? You remember the name — Dominique Ettori."

Sena followed him outside and put five bullets through his body before he was chased and arrested.

On him they found an old newspaper, dated September 1922, giving an account of Ettori's trial and acquittal for the murder of Sena.

The matter was of little interest to me, but it gives a sidelight upon the relentless pertinacity of the Corsican vendetta.

The other incident that took place at about the same time was of vital importance to me, and however long I am permitted to live, I shall never quite get over it.

During the ten months since Caviglioli's death and my removal to the Ridge of Death, Antoinette Leca had been my constant companion and adviser.

It has been said of me that, with my passionate nature, any woman of mine led a life that was a miniature hell on earth. It is a lie, of course, though the quarrels I had with Mimi probably lent color to these stories.

But Antoinette Leca was an entirely different woman from Mimi. I did not love Mimi, though I admired her enormously and she stirred my passion as no other woman has ever done. But love her — no! Now I loved Antoinette Leca and I admired her, too: not only for her beauty, but for her bravery and her commonsense wisdom. She was not brilliant, perhaps; but her suggestions, though simple and obvious once they had been made, were always reliable. When I acted upon her advice I never went wrong. She was a good comrade, too; never nagging, always ready to help, never complaining, never blaming.

Even when her child was expected I could not persuade her to return to civilization.

"No," she insisted, "I am of the banditti, and you—you are the King of the Maquis. Would you have your son born in a village?"

We were certain that it would be a son, and had even decided upon the name, André Luigi.

"When I am gone," I used to say, "André Luigi will take my place. We must teach him early to shoot and to ride and to command."

Then, one day as summer was slipping away into autumn, Antoinette Leca's time came. This was something outside my experience: I was dreadfully frightened and worried.

"We must have a doctor," I told Pietro. "Take some of the men and fetch one from Ajaccio."

"*Si, siore.* But if the doctor refuses to come?"

"Offer him this," I said, giving Pietro a large bag of money.

Pietro chewed his tobacco meditatively.

"And if the doctor still refuses to come?"

"*Madre di Dios!*" I cried. "Don't you realize it's urgent? If the doctor will not come you must bring him. Understand?"

Pietro nodded as he swung himself up into the saddle.

"*Si, siore,*" he said. "We shall bring one."

He succeeded, but I shall never forget the agony of waiting.

I thought Antoinette Leca would die, and so, I believe, did the doctor. However, she lived, and so for a while did André Luigi.

No father can ever have been prouder of his son than I was of mine. I saw in him my successor.

But the gods had deserted me. André Luigi lived but fifteen days. Perhaps the cold of the mountains was too much for him.

No, I shall never get over it; nor, I think, will Antoinette Leca.

She was so ill and changed after the child's death that I sent her down from the mountains to one of the villages, foolishly believing that the police would not trouble her.

XXII

Although for a while the authorities relaxed their attempts at wiping me out, so that I had almost come to believe that they were going to leave me in peace, as the autumn of 1932 drew on they again began an intensive siege. Troops and gendarmes that had been recalled to France were once more sent across and the old game of hide-and-seek began in earnest.

What had caused this intensification of the siege of the Maquis I do not know. Possibly explanations had been demanded by the Paris newspapers as to why a force of six hundred men, fitted out with the most up-to-date fighting equipment, had failed for a whole year to dislodge a bandit and his followers, who probably numbered no more than two hundred, from the mountains.

News was brought to me in about November that the French Government had offered a reward of a hundred thousand francs for my capture—or death. To a poverty-ridden peasantry this amount of money must have seemed a fortune. I wonder how many turned over in their minds the idea of selling me? It would have been possible for quite a number of them to have devised a scheme by which the police could have got me into an awkward position. A really clever man, by a series of false information to my guides, might have gained this reward. Yet only one made this attempt. Whether it was from fear of the reprisals I would undoubtedly take if they failed in their attempt to betray me, or whether it was from a feeling of loyalty to a man who had been a good friend to them in the past and who might be useful to them in the future, I do not know. The fact remains that only this one man made the attempt and he gained his reward—though not the one he expected.

It was one of my guides who first brought me news of this man's treachery. He had obtained the news from one of my spies in Lopigna, the same one who had helped me trace Mimi and Giocundi to the cinema on the unfortunate night when I shot the woodcutter's uncle and his mistress.

The traitor was an innkeeper of Lopigna and, so my spies' report went, he had gone to the Prefect of Police in Ajaccio and offered to betray me and a number of my men provided that the reward was doubled.

I had often used this man's inn as a meeting place where I entertained those of my women who were not living at my stronghold in the mountains. The plan he had suggested to the Prefect of Police in Ajaccio was that on the next occasion I entertained one of my women at his inn, a messenger was to be sent to Ajaccio, when a posse of police would at once be dispatched to the inn to arrest me in bed! The poor fool, did he imagine the police would ever catch me sleeping?

The final details of this plan I received from rather an unusual source—a well-to-do business man of Ajaccio who had been paying me for protection. I relied, as a rule, upon the peasantry for my intelligence. It seemed odd getting a warning from a wealthy merchant. The explanation, however, was quite simple. A great deal of interest was being taken in Ajaccio, Corte, Bastia, and the other chief centers in the attempts to capture me. The Corsican loves a gamble, and there were many bets laid on or against the police ever catching me. The merchant who sent me warning of the trap that was being set at the Lopigna inn stood to lose a large amount if I were caught. It is not surprising, then, that he sent me a warning that was as acceptable to me as if it had been prompted by kindness instead of an effort to protect his own pocket.

Marchi, when he betrayed me, had paid the penalty, and so had Castiglione after he had betrayed Romanetti. And when Arna Goscapi had shot his leader in the back I had seen to it that he, too, not only paid for his treachery but provided a warning to anyone else similarly minded. It is the only way in the Maquis. You cannot manage a couple of hundred men with a pair of kid gloves. One has to rule by fear, and any softness of heart is taken as a sign of weakness. A bandit leader cannot afford to be thought weak. Thus, not only for my own satisfaction, but for the morale of my men, the innkeeper of Lopigna had to pay the price of his greed and foolhardiness.

I set to work and mapped out a plan by which the innkeeper would incriminate himself. Not that I doubted either of my informants. Rather I have a sense of justice, a trait that I shared with Romanetti, that demands a man shall have a sporting chance. It was this sense of justice that prompted Romanetti to put a gun into Castiglione's hand, and so almost brought about his own death. It was for the same reason that I gave Goscapi his fighting chance. Now, I decided, this precious innkeeper should be given the opportunity of putting his head into the noose.

With this idea in my mind I sent a messenger to Antoinette Leca to meet me at the inn the following night.

Accordingly the next evening I set off with a large escort, arriving at the inn about midnight. Leaving my men in concealment outside, I entered and was at once shown into the room where Antoinette Leca was waiting for me. I lowered the light and, in a whisper, explained the position to her.

"The son of a dog has sold me," I told her. "Already one of his men will be on the way to Ajaccio to fetch the police."

Antoinette Leca started up in a panic. She was never scared of what might happen to her, but if any danger threatened me she would at once begin to worry.

"Then what are you doing here? *Dio mio*, André! Have you suddenly become mad?"

"Ssh! Not so loud, *ma petite*. They may hear and everything will be spoiled. In a few moments we shall leave the inn by this window and join my men in the bush—then for a little amusement. *Hein?*"

Antoinette smiled at me as though I were a small boy and she my mother.

"*Nom d'un chien*, André! You are a strange one. Why didn't you shoot the fellow outright instead of going in for all this playacting?"

I tried to explain my point of view, but she could not see it. If I were satisfied that the innkeeper was guilty, then what was the use of playing with fire? No, you cannot argue with a woman. I soon gave up the attempt.

As soon as I thought it was safe to do so we climbed out of the window. I had chosen the room carefully because of an outhouse with a lean-to roof that came to within two feet of the sill. It was an easy matter to reach the ground by way of this roof. I slid down first, very silently, and was ready to receive Antoinette into my arms when she followed. Five minutes after leaving the room we were seated in the undergrowth beside my men.

It was about half an hour later that one of my guides arrived. He had been stationed farther down the Ajaccio road to watch for the arrival of the police.

He reported that there were a couple of dozen of them and that they had dismounted and, leaving their horses, were proceeding as silently as possible on foot towards the inn.

A few minutes later the police came into sight, and while half their number surrounded the inn to cut off my escape, the other half were admitted by the innkeeper himself. We waited expectantly.

Suddenly there came a loud hammering on a door, obviously that of the room where Antoinette Leca and I were supposed to be, and the *brigadier*'s voice, very clear in the stillness:

"*Ouvrez!* In the name of the Republic!"

Then silence, followed by the splintering of woodwork as the door was burst in.

I could picture the police as they entered the deserted room. They would have their guns drawn and they would be treading delicately, like a cat on a wet floor, expecting every minute a burst of firing from the guns of the most feared man in Corsica. But nothing came.

I would have given a lot to have seen their faces when they found the room empty and to have heard what the *brigadier* said to the innkeeper. That he did not believe the man's story I gathered from his remarks as they left the inn. No doubt he considered that the whole thing was a plant on the innkeeper's part to extract money from the police, for the traitor had demanded a portion of the reward in advance.

How I longed to be able to turn our guns on the police as they passed, a thoroughly disgruntled crew, on their return journey to Ajaccio: we could have shot them down like rats; not one of them would have lived to take the story back to Ajaccio. But the innkeeper was my game, and I was afraid that in the commotion that followed our opening fire on the police he might escape. To my way of thinking, the death of two dozen police would not compensate me if the wretched traitor slipped through my fingers.

Impatiently I waited until my guide returned with the information that the police had mounted and set off in the direction of Ajaccio at a sharp canter.

Even then I gave them time to get well on their way before interviewing my friend, the landlord.

I had made certain, however, by throwing a cordon of my men about it, that he could not leave the inn. I reckoned that he would realize that I had been warned and was planning to make his getaway before I returned to pay the debt I owed

I heard afterwards that he had begged the police to let him accompany them, but that they had been so incensed at being tricked, and, believing that his fear was only playacting for their benefit, they had refused his request. They even warned him that if he did accompany them to Ajaccio it would be under arrest on a charge of having obtained money from the Prefect of Police under false pretences. It would have been better for him if they had arrested him, but probably he supposed that I would not remain near the inn, knowing that the police were coming. He thought that he would be able to make his escape before I returned.

One of my men caught him as he crept out through the back door, his money and his few valuables in a bag.

I have never seen a man so overcome by terror as he was. His teeth were rattling together and his face twitching. Every now and then his arms, or legs, or neck would give a violent jerk as though he were a marionette and the showman had clumsily jerked the string.

He made a pitiable attempt at bluffing it out.

"Well, Monsieur Spada, you had a narrow squeak. It is fortunate that you took my warning and left so quickly."

"Your warning?"

The man twisted his face into a terrified grin.

"Why, yes. Didn't you hear me knock at your door and tell you that the police were coming? I thought that was why you and Madame had left."

"So you knocked at my door to warn me?"

"*Mais certainement—*"

"It is strange that I didn't hear you."

"It must have been after you had gone, Monsieur Spada. But so long as you are safe that is all that matters. Now if you will excuse me—"

I smiled at him. But I do not think he found my smile reassuring. In the light of our lanterns I saw his eyes rolling, like I have seen the eyes of a trapped animal roll.

"*Un moment, mon ami.* There is no hurry, surely? I have seen little of you lately, and I have a feeling that I shall see still less of you after tonight. Now tell me, that is a fine tree you have over there."

His eyes followed the direction of my finger.

"*Mais oui*, Monsieur. An oak. It is very old."

"And that big limb, jutting out there, how high from the ground do you think it is?"

He considered.

"Fifteen feet, perhaps, Monsieur Spada. But, *je vous prie*, let me start on my way. I have a sick sister in Bologna. I have promised to visit her."

"*Eh bien*, I shall not keep you long now. I am sure your sick sister would not wish to be disturbed at four o'clock in the morning. Now, that branch on the oak, will it, think you, hold the weight of a man?"

The innkeeper looked at it again while I watched the sweat breaking out on his forehead.

"*Peut-être*, Monsieur, but I should say not. Now, forgive me if I go. My sister is very sick. I should have visited her last evening but for your arrival."

"You think then it wouldn't bear the weight of a man, say as heavy as you?"

I could see from his eyes that the miserable man had about come to the end of his tether.

"How could I say?" he cried wildly. "I do not know what you mean."

"It is just a matter of curiosity," I explained. "*Maintenant*, shall we have a small bet upon it? *Dix francs?* You say that bough will not hold the weight of a man—I say, yes. We shall try. Antoine, bring a rope."

The innkeeper threw himself on the ground, tearing at his greasy black hair with tortured fingers.

"Monsieur Spada, I swear that I had nothing to do with the coming of the police. On my brother's grave, I swear it."

"And who said you had?" I asked pleasantly. "Ah, here is Antoine with the rope. Antoine, throw the rope across that bough *là. Alors, mon ami,* if that limb does not sustain your weight—why, I shall owe you ten francs. *Venez!*"

Kicking and screaming, he was led to the oak, underneath which some of the men had set a water butt. His arms were tied and, with great difficulty, he was lifted on to the butt and the rope adjusted. A second rope had been tied to the barrel, the other end of which was attached to Pietro's saddle.

"*Etes-vous prêt,* Pietro?" I called. "*Un—deux—trois—*"

The bough held. I had won my bet. But somehow the innkeeper was not in a position to pay. To even things up I decided to burn his inn, and this we did, after having pinned a paper to the man's coat upon which was written a warning to all others that a similar fate awaited them should they attempt to make money out of my death or capture.

I would like to have stayed to watch the inn burnt to the ground, but I was afraid that the flames might attract the police. Regretfully, I gave the order to return to camp.

A strong wind had risen and was thrashing the flames into a fury. As we entered the Maquis I paused and turned back in my saddle.

The big oak was silhouetted against the burning house, and as the wind tore up the valley a figure danced and bobbed beneath the bare branches, its feet a yard from the ground.

XXIII

There were no further attempts by any of the peasants to gain the reward offered for my capture. Possibly, the example I had made of the innkeeper of Lopigna deterred any who might have felt that way inclined. I prefer to think, however, that the peasantry as a whole remained true to me. The Lopigna innkeeper was not a Corsican: he was French. That, of course, made a vast difference. But there was one Corsican who joined Vazi and the police in their attempts to capture me. This was Giocundi.

I was not surprised when I heard from one of my guides that Giocundi had returned to Corsica and was planning to hunt me even as I had hunted him. Neither did I blame him.

In a way he was more to be feared than Vazi. True, he hadn't Vazi's quick brain and fearless spirit, but he knew the Maquis as well as Vazi did and he knew my habits and haunts better. Vazi, though he had been brought up in and near the Maquis, had spent some years in Nice as a gendarme. Giocundi had never left Corsica until my vendetta had recently driven him out.

He had been a friend of Romanetti and later of myself, though I would not call him a friend; rather he had attached himself to my band.

To the police he would be invaluable, and this knowledge must have given him great pleasure. It could not have been pleasant for him to be hunted as I had hunted him. Now that there was a chance of having his revenge he must have been enormously glad.

What he had done with Mimi I was unable to find out. Probably he had brought her back with him to Ajaccio. Now I was penned up in the mountains there was little chance of my carrying out my vendetta.

One of his first acts—and this must have given him an unholy joy—was to bring about the arrest of Antoinette Leca. He must have known how dear she was to me.

They had nothing against her beyond her association with me. Giocundi arranged the whole scheme. He must have convinced the authorities that Antoinette Leca knew of my movements and that she could be made to talk: even, possibly, bribed to betray me.

He had discovered where I had hidden her, and one night a posse of police, with Giocundi acting as guide, had arrived at her house and removed her to Ajaccio.

Giocundi must have realized that Antoinette could never be made to talk and contrived the arrest purely with the idea of spiting me. But if the authorities had imagined that they were going to get any information out of her, they were disappointed.

How I cursed myself that I had not foreseen her arrest, and kept her in the mountains with me. It was only with the idea of protecting her that I had insisted on her return to civilization. Instead of protecting her, I had landed her in prison.

Gradually, as the winter came on, the police closed in upon the Ridge of Death. I still believed it invulnerable so long as I was able to obtain supplies of provisions and ammunition. That was my only fear—that we would be starved out. And bit by bit I saw this coming about.

Either I had underestimated Giocundi or my pursuit of him had put such terror into him that he had become imbued with a new spirit. Before, he had always been wily in a sly, sneaking fashion; now, he appeared to have developed an intelligence I would not have believed him to possess.

He knew my hiding places. He knew the vantage points where my outposts were generally set. He knew the various "dumps" where friendly peasants left provisions and ammunition for us. And so it was made possible for the police to penetrate nearer to my fort, and, in some instances, to surprise and shoot down the outposts. Again and again we found our caches rifled, so that we began to run short of both food and ammunition. The lack of provisions would not have mattered so greatly in the summer, for then game would have been plentiful. But in midwinter, when many of the animals had been forced down to the lowlands in search of food, and the yield of our goat herd had fallen low, this lack of supplies had a very demoralizing effect upon some of my men.

And so it was that I found my band of followers gradually shrinking. The newcomers, who had served under Caviglioli and Bartoli, were the first to go. Then the rout spread to my men, and in twos and threes they disappeared, beginning with the less faithful members.

In a way this eased the position, for there were many less stomachs to fill. But that was the only bright spot in a very black prospect. The lack of food and the desertions of their comrades was undermining the morale of those who remained. Add to this the bitter cold of a winter in the mountains, and the constant strain under which they lived: no wonder some of them cracked up.[15] Sickness was not an enemy we ever took into consideration in the Maquis, but last winter[16] it took its toll of the Ridge of Death.

It seemed that the gods had forsaken us entirely. Above us the heavens frowned down with snow-heavy clouds. About us was the bitter blight of winter. Beneath us the police and the military, like a great flock of vultures watching a dying man.

Then, one morning early, there came the dull rattle of machine-gun fire, chattering over the frozen snow.

---

[15] A foreshadowing of what will happen to Spada himself.
[16] This gives us an idea of when the account was recorded.

I lay for a moment listening. It was nearer than any firing I had previously heard. Slipping on my boots and cloak, I went out into the compound.

It was not yet dawn, but there was about the mountainside that cold, grey light that ushers in the winter day.

A number of my men were grouped along the stone breastworks talking in low voices. I joined them.

Pietro looked up at my approach.

"They're coming up fast," he remarked. "Antoine says that a couple of hundred soldiers were moved up from Ajaccio in the night. I've put out a cordon to try and hold them back. But a man can't fight on an empty stomach in this cold."

"They're being pushed back?"

"If there are any of them left to push back," said Pietro.

Gradually they straggled in, our front line, many wounded, all practically frozen.

"Who the hell can fight like this?" growled one. "*Madre di Dios!* I would rather be in Ajaccio gaol. I would at least be warm and have a little food in my belly. Those soldiers, they were given hot soup before they attacked. I could smell it from where I lay. Why stay here to be shot down? I'm getting out of it."

There were growls of agreement from all about him. I could see that the rout had set in. Men were collecting their bundles together; talking in low voices as to the best places to make for. The garrison of the Ridge of Death was dispersing.

By threats and persuasion I might have got them to remain. But what would have been the use? The cold and the lack of food had beaten them, besides which, our supplies of ammunition had fallen so low that I was doubtful of our being able to with- stand a heavy siege.

It was better to go before the morale of the men was thoroughly broken. A strategic retreat is one thing: a thorough rout is another.

Calling to the men, I suggested that it would be best to evacuate the fort and take up a new position in the mountain caves. I did not intend to leave the fort for good: once we were thoroughly rested we could retake it and drive the soldiers back into the Maquis.

A number of the men agreed to my idea; others decided that they were going to try their luck farther away from the Ridge of Death. I suppose they felt that I was the jam that was attracting the military wasps, and that it would be safer to put a few hundred square miles in between themselves and the centre of trouble.

Having decided to abandon the fort, the quicker we carried out our retreat the better. Once it was light we could not have made our escape into the mountains.

And so it was, when the cold grey light of morning had crept down the snow-clad slopes of Monte d'Oro and entered the Maquis, that the military took possession of my fort on the Ridge of Death without a shot being fired.

I deeply regretted the evacuation of my stronghold, for it was a further sign of my waning power. But almost more than this I regretted having to leave behind some of my most treasured possessions. There was the letter that the Englishwoman had sent me when she sailed. I hated leaving that, for I had often read it and been reminded of her visit. Then, too, there were many souvenirs of Mimi. I had hated her for her betrayal of me, but that did not prevent my having very pleasant memories of our early days together.

Most of Antoinette Leca's possessions had been transferred to her house when she left the mountains, but, even so, there were still odd little reminders of her that I had treasured.

I suppose it is the way of lovers all the world over; they like to have some little thing to remind them of the girl they once loved — a handkerchief, a glove, a dance program, a slipper, a silk stocking. Even though their love has long since grown cold, when they turn over these relics they can whip up the thrill of some of their old memories with the lash of sentiment. I suppose I must have had boxes full of these souvenirs of the girls I had loved, and who had loved me.

These were not my only "relics." In one corner of my hut I had stacked the rifles I had taken from my enemies, mostly belonging to gendarmes and soldiers. On the walls I had hung their revolvers, a *kepi* or two, and various other items of their accoutrements.

I hated leaving my "museum" and its "exhibits"; but it would have been impossible to take it with me.

Though I had been driven from my stronghold and had been deserted by the majority of my band, I did not for a moment consider myself beaten.

The police killed both Caviglioli and Bartoli, but nobody should ever kill or capture me. Of this I was perfectly confident. The time would come when the military and the police would tire of chasing shadows and the expedition would be recalled. Then I intended to collect my men together again, and my rule of the Maquis would begin where I had left off, only strengthened by the failure of the authorities to capture me. Meanwhile, I had to be content to be hunted like a *mufro* about the mountains. I made several attempts to dislodge the soldiers from the Ridge of Death, but, with my depleted forces, I was unsuccessful.

Gradually the rest of my men drifted away till I was left with no more than half a dozen. There were Pietro and Antoine and Farozza, the Italian, and three others. Even these were soon to be separated from me.

Christmas came and went, and January slowly dragged past. The cold was very intense, even for me who had been used to it for so many years. I suppose it was largely the lack of sufficient food, proper housing and fires. I had spent ten winters in the mountains and had felt no ill effects from the cold, but then I had the shelter of my hut with its stone walls a couple of feet thick, and had never been without a fire in the really cold weather. Now it was rarely safe to light a fire for fear of giving our position away to the soldiers. An inadequate supply of food was another difficulty and our store of ammunition was getting dangerously low. Naturally there was no means of weighing oneself in the mountains, but I am certain that it is no exaggeration when I say that I lost at least thirty pounds in weight during the early months of the year.

Then, one day in early February, when the winter seemed to be relenting of its attempts to freeze us to death and the heat of a very welcome sun was penetrating to our bones, I decided upon an expedition into the Maquis in search of game.

We were skirting the edge of a thickly wooded ravine, down the centre of which roared one of the many mountain streams in spate with snow water. Pietro and I were together, having separated from the others. Suddenly, from a patch of shrub about fifty yards to our right there came the crackle of rifle fire.

Pietro doubled up and rolled down the bank into the ravine. I followed his example, though I had not been hit. He landed on a ledge about twenty feet above the stream.

The ravine, like many others in the mountains, was honeycombed with caves. There was one not many yards from where Pietro had fallen. Seizing him under the armpits, I backed into it, dragging him with me. A moment later I heard the rattle of loose stones as the men who had shot at us descended the side of the ravine.

Having propped Pietro up against a boulder near the back of the cave, I crept forward and chose a spot from which I could cover the cave's mouth.

Almost immediately the head of an unwary gendarme appeared around the corner, and, firing quickly, I had the pleasure of seeing him stagger back and, after windmilling with his arms for a moment, pitch over into the stream.

For a while the gendarmes kept firing at the cave mouth from a distance. There was no hope of getting a direct shot at me without exposing themselves, but there was a chance that one of their shots, ricocheting on the stone sides of the cave, might find me. Finally they grew tired of this.

I had crawled back to where Pietro lay, and, while still keeping an eye on the cave mouth, made an examination of his wound.

The bullet had got him in the stomach and he was bleeding pretty freely. Tearing up his shirt, I bound him up as well as I could.

He was in great pain and almost unconscious.

"How's that?" I asked him, when I had finished my rough doctoring. "Anything you want?"

He seemed to rouse himself up a little.

"Drink?" he said.

For some time I had been unconsciously listening to the tinkle of water in the far corner of the cave. Removing my hat, I groped my way towards the sound.

There was a small pool of very cold water that had percolated through from the hillside and was dripping, a drop at a time, from the roof.

Filling my hat from the pool, I returned to Pietro.

For a moment, as I stooped to collect the water, my eyes had been off the entrance to the cave; in that moment one of the gendarmes had crept forward and was standing, his rifle raised ready to shoot, but uncertain of his aim on account of the darkness within the cave.

I dropped my hatful of water and, snatching out a gun, shot from my hip.

The gendarme gave a kind of choking cough, and subsided where he lay.

I did not know whether he was killed or only badly wounded, and I did not intend to find out. Anyway, I kept my gun in my hand as I returned to the pool for more water, for I expected that the gendarme's comrades would probably attempt to remove him from where he lay, in case he were still alive.

The water revived Pietro. He even tried to laugh.

"We seem nicely corked up here," he remarked. "What are you expecting to do?"

"Stay here till they get tired of waiting, and you are fit enough to move."

He coughed with a funny gasping sound.

"You will have to wait a long time then, *mon ami*, for I'm not going to get over this. They've got me this time."

I tried to convince him that he was going to recover, but I made a poor job of it, for I knew as well as he did that he was through.

"Wait till it's dark," he whispered, "then slip past them. If you roll a couple of stones down to draw their fire you could make it."

"And leave you?"

"*Pourquoi non?* I shall never leave this cave. Why should you die watching over a dead man?"

It was growing dusk outside. I could barely see the figure of the fallen gendarme. He had not moved.

Of a sudden the head and shoulders of a man appeared above the body in the cave mouth. One of the gendarmes had risked coming to the help of his friend. A moment later there were two bodies, instead of one, lying amongst the boulders. The rest of the gendarmes set up a howl of rage. I have no doubt but that they would have lynched me if only they could have got me out into the open.

Slowly the grey mouth of the cave deepened into blackness. Behind me I could hear the harsh, uneven breathing of Pietro. An owl was hooting down the ravine, a weird, echoing cry. The stream roared and rattled over the stones.

There came Pietro's voice, very small in the sound-filled night:

"... *Ami* ... *sacré bleu!* ... the pain ..."

I crawled back to where he lay.

"Is there anything you want?" I asked.

I could feel his hand groping up my arm.

"*Mais oui.* Have you a plug of tobacco?"

I cut him a piece and found his hand.

"Have you got it?"

"*Si, Siore.*"

I returned to my guard over the entrance. From behind me I could hear the faint sound of Pietro chewing his plug.

At last he gave a deep sigh.

"All right, Pietro?"

"*Si, si.* I think I will sleep a little."

There are perhaps a dozen memories that are stamped upon my mind more deeply than any, so that when I close my eyes at night, they float up before me like the mist from the hollows on a frosty night. One is Mimi, glaring into my eyes while a beam of light strikes upon my stiletto as it lies between us; another is the scent of that purple climbing plant that brings back the memory of Marita; and yet another is that night in the cave with the roar of the stream below and, close behind me, the quick, uneasy breathing of Pietro.

Presently only the sound of the stream filled the night with its restless voice, and I did not need to place my hand beneath Pietro's coat to learn I had lost a very true friend.

I was now free to make my escape from the cave. That it would be best to make the attempt at once I was certain. Before long it would be lighter, and once the darkest part of the night was gone I would have to remain where I was until the following night. I had no desire to spend a day there. If the gendarmes had the sense to think of it, a few grenades would soon get me out of the cave or bury me beneath a fall of rock.

Pietro had suggested rolling some stones down the bank to mislead the gendarmes. The idea seemed as good as any. I crept to the mouth of the cave and, choosing a couple of boulders of the size I wanted, I set them rolling to the left. At once a volley of shots rang out.

As quick as any *mufro* I darted out and leapt up the side of the ravine to the right. My life in the mountains had made me as quick-footed as a wild sheep, but, even so, I slipped in the darkness and rolled down the slope.

Luckily, I was only bruised when I came to rest almost at the edge of the stream. Above me I could hear the gendarmes moving about and cursing lustily.

Very probably my fall had saved me. The gendarmes seemed entirely to have lost track of me, and I was now so close to the stream that the sound of the water drowned any noise I made.

I kept close to the stream for about half a mile; then, certain that I had shaken off the hunt, I cut up through the trees and, by the time the first grey light of morning was filtering through the heavy snow clouds, I crept into one of my hiding places on the mountain.

XXIV

Throughout the rest of February and March I was entirely alone.

My band had become split up and was spread over the island in twos and threes, as had been the old way of the bandits before the big leaders, such as Romanetti, Caviglioli, Bartoli and myself, had collected large numbers of them under one leadership. Many had been killed and others had been captured. For myself, I had no fear of being caught. The peasantry was still upon my side. So long as I was free in the Maquis I could count upon food and ammunition and even, at times, shelter.

It was my boast that with all their aircraft, machine guns, armored cars and tanks, the military would never run me to earth. And it was not a vain boast, for during those months they realized that they could never bring about my arrest or death. It was only by taking advantage of my one weakness that they finally got me behind bars.

During those early months of the year I was never without a friend, and as often as not it was a woman who helped me.

For some time the longing had been growing in me to see my parents again. In the days before the expedition against the banditti had landed in Corsica I had visited them often; but for the previous eighteen months I had seen but little of them.

Some years before they had moved from Lopigna, where I had spent my boyhood, to Coggia, the village in which Romanetti's wife had lived. At Coggia they had bought a small farm some little way out of the village itself. It was a fairly safe place to visit, for the house stood in its own fields well away from other dwellings, and my arrival would not be likely to be noticed.

As the winter receded and spring drew on, this "homesickness" for a home in which I had never lived grew more intense.

Finally, it became so strong that I decided to risk capture and spend Easter with my parents. My resolve was strengthened by the news that the commander of the expedition had sent in a report to Paris that it was impossible to take me.

April came, and finally on the night of April 12th I crept out of the Maquis and across the fields to my parents' house.

They were asleep when I arrived, but I easily found a way into the house and awakened them.

They were just as pleased as ever to see me. I have often been asked whether my being a bandit made any difference to my parents' feelings for me. I can definitely say that it did not. Though I was an outcast from civilization, one who was banned by the law—for that word "banned" is, I believe, the derivation of the term "bandit"[17]—I was always welcomed at my parents' house. Even, I think, they were a little proud of the power their son wielded in the island.

A Northerner, so I believe, looks upon any man who is against the law as being a criminal. That is not the Corsican's point of view. I suppose it is the outcome of our age-old system of the vendetta. A man who fails to avenge his honor is despised by our nation. But if he does avenge an injury done to him or his, and in doing so kills a man, he is outside the law. He has received the *Sonetto*, that is, he has been outlawed. His fellow Corsicans do not consider him a criminal. He has killed in defense of his honor. He would stand far lower in their estimation if he had failed to kill. It is the vendetta, that institution that France would stamp out if she could.

So it was that, though a couple of peaceable Americans might feel bitterly ashamed of having a notorious gangster as a son, my parents felt no shame in owning the "King of the Maquis" as their son.

---

[17] Actually, "ban" is derived from the Old Norse *banna*, "to prohibit, curse." "Bandit" derives from the Italian *bandito*: "One who is banished."

Soon after the commander of the expedition against the banditti had sent in his report that it was impossible to take me, a remarkably handsome girl presented herself at the *Prefecture de Police* in Marseilles and asked to speak privately with the Prefect.

Naturally, I knew nothing of this at the time. It was from what I was told later, partly by the girl herself, and partly by a journalist when I was in prison, that I have been able to piece together the events that led up to my arrest.

This girl was Antoinette Ricci, daughter of the mail driver whom I had shot near Lopigna when the mails contract had been taken from me.

Antoinette was only about seventeen at the time of her father's death, but she had sworn that when the time came she would be avenged upon me.

She had followed the reports of the expedition and had realized, as soon as anybody, that I would never be taken by force. Then she saw her chance. She knew that my one great weakness was a beautiful woman: she knew that she had grown into a beautiful woman. How simple, then, to try her wiles on me and, once I was well and truly "hooked," deliver me up to the authorities.

That was the plan she set before the Prefect of Police in Marseilles.

The reward, she told him, was nothing to her. It was revenge she wanted for the killing of her father.

The Prefect must have thought well of the idea, for he sent to Ajaccio for the *Sûreté* detectives who had been attached to the expedition. On their arrival in Marseilles the scheme was thoroughly gone into and finally accepted. Antoinette Ricci was sent to Ajaccio under the escort of a couple of detectives. Using an assumed name she took rooms in one of the hotels and started planning how to get into touch with me.

For a man this would probably have been impossible: for a pretty woman most things are possible. Within a week Antoinette Ricci had become friendly with one of my spies and had persuaded him to try and arrange a meeting between her and me.

I don't blame my spy. It was with no idea that he was helping in my betrayal that he brought Antoinette Ricci's message tome. He was as much deceived by her as I was later.

It was just after Easter and I was still at my father's farm when Paoli came in search of me.

"Madre di Dios!" he exclaimed. "Such a one, André! Such a beauty you have never seen."

"Well," I asked, "what of it?"

Paoli grinned at me.

"You are a lucky one, André. This beauty, she has fallen for you. She is not the first either, *hein?* She wishes to meet the great André Spada of whom she has heard so much. *Voyez!* Here is her photograph."

I took it from him. The girl was certainly beautiful, with her big dark eyes and full figure.

"She is as nice as that?" I asked.

Paoli kissed a hand in the direction of Ajaccio and rolled his eyes expressively.

"*Par bleu!* A thousand times prettier. In this picture you cannot see how her eyes sparkle, and how red her lips are."

"And the girl's name?"

"Germaine Ducrois. And you will agree to see her, *n'est-ce-que pas?*"

I looked at the photograph again. Germaine was really lovely—just the type of girl I admire. And it is rather flattering, too, to have a request such as this from one so good-looking as Germaine Ducrois.

"You do not think that it is a trap?" I asked Paoli.

"*Mais non.* She is French, it is true. But she knows few people in Ajaccio and none of the police or military."

"Very well," I agreed. "I will meet Mlle. Ducrois, but we must take precautions in case it is a trick of the police, as I do not know the girl."

Though my band had been temporarily broken up, with the slackening of the military's attempts to capture me some of my men had returned and I still had a number of spies, such as Paoli, who, though not outlaws themselves, were as much to be trusted as my own men.

I agreed with Paoli upon a meeting place and arranged to have the spot watched for some while before we were due there. "Germaine" was not to be told of the position of our rendezvous. She was to meet Paoli in Ajaccio and accompany him. As a further safeguard I instructed a number of my spies to watch Paoli and the girl to make certain that she was not being followed at a distance by the police. As a final precaution I arrived nearly an hour late.

Antoinette—for I cannot think of her as Germaine, though that was the name I knew her as—was just as charming as Paoli had described her, and we spent a very pleasant evening together. She wanted to know about my life in the Maquis, and listened very attentively to my stories. I even told her of how I 'had shot Ricci, her father; but she had herself under such perfect control that she showed no more interest in this event than in any of the others I recounted.

That was the first of many meetings. No doubt Antoinette realized that I was a careful bird and had decided to get me well into her net before closing it.

I still took precautions, but, as I grew to know and trust Antoinette, I was not so careful. Most of our meetings took place about my father's farm, in a hut or a stable; but I rang the changes carefully. One night it would be the hut, another the Maquis, even, once, I took her to dance at the café of a man who was in my pay. Antoinette would never know where we were to meet the following night. Every time I went through the same precautions, drawing a cordon around our meeting place to prevent an ambush, and detailing a secret escort to follow Antoinette and Paoli.

At last, upon the first day of May, I made the mistake that led to my capture and imprisonment.

Antoinette and I had met in a hut on the farm. Perhaps it was the spring in my blood, or perhaps the girl's lovemaking was not altogether a sham as it had at first been. Whatever the reason, Antoinette Ricci seemed more beautiful and desirable than ever before.

As we were parting I asked:

"And tomorrow night, *Mignonne*?"

"*Ah oui*, André, of course."

I released her gently from my arms.

"*Alors, à demain*—in this hut, *chérie*?"

She nodded, looking up at me with her dark eyes.

"*Mais oui*, in this hut at eight o'clock."

Dreaming of our next meeting, I watched her go. If only I had known that at last she had gained what she wanted—a definite meeting place. She went straight back to her hotel, and later, dressed as a chambermaid, she slipped out at the back of the building and told the Prefect of Police that he could make his arrangements—that by the following evening André Spada would either be dead or in gaol.

It shows how completely I had come under her spell that I did not trouble to take my usual precautions, with the result that the police were able to throw a cordon round the hut in readiness for my arrival. Machine guns were brought up and placed where they could command the various tracks to the hut: one, even, was trained on the door. So the stage was set for my entry, and Antoinette Ricci, my betrayer, was waiting for me in the hut to see the fulfillment of her revenge.

Then a strange thing happened. Or perhaps it was not so strange when one remembers the power I always had over women's hearts.

As Antoinette Ricci waited for my death or, almost worse, the final degradation of my arrest, she suddenly realized that she did not want me to be killed or arrested. She wanted me to live and to be free, and for her to be with me.

She had begun by playing at love so that she might betray me, and now, when it was too late, she realized that what she had been playacting had become a real and terrible fact—that, now it was too late, she loved me.

There was one comparatively safe route from the Maquis to the hut where Antoinette was waiting. She guessed that I would come this way. During the last two weeks we had often gone along it, so that she knew it well.

Darting out into the open Antoinette made for the Maquis. The police, taken by surprise, let her go. No doubt they did not realize that she had undergone a sudden change of heart. They had been told that she was to be given a free hand in her arrangements for my capture; but they must have been very puzzled by her sudden change of tactics.

Coming down the mountain path that led towards the hut through the dense growth of the Maquis I saw her coming. Her hair was tumbled about her shoulders and her blouse had been torn by the thorns as she thrust her way through the undergrowth. Tears streamed down her cheeks and her mouth was distorted by fear.

"André!" she was crying. "André! The police! Oh, where are you, André? *Madre di Dios!* Can't you hear me, André? The police!"

I answered her, and a moment later she was sobbing in my arms.

"What is it, *ma petite*?" I asked.

"The police! They have the hut surrounded. Quick! Back to the mountains—take me with you—" But we were too late. One of the gendarmes had followed Antoinette to find out what she was doing. He now stood some little way down the path, a look of triumph on his face, as he carefully sighted his rifle upon me.

With a wild scream Antoinette threw herself forward in between me and the gendarme. At that moment he fired.

Antoinette put her hand to her side with a puzzled look on her face.

It was the last shot that gendarme ever fired. My revolver barked twice and he fell in a twisted heap at the side of the track.

Fortunately, he was the only one to have followed the girl, but I knew that our shots would soon bring a swarm of his fellows yapping after us.

Antoinette had sunk to her knees and was dabbing in a dazed sort of way at her side with a handkerchief that was rapidly becoming dyed crimson.

There was no time to examine her wound. At any moment the police would appear. I could already hear them below in the Maquis calling for their dead comrade. Antoinette was a big girl, but I was still strong in spite of the lean winter I had had.

I lifted her in my arms and set off for one of my hiding places in the mountains. At this Antoinette roused herself.

"Put me down, André," she begged. "Alone you can escape easily. Sure as death they will catch you if you try to carry me with you."

I refused.

"Do you think I would leave you when you have saved my life?"

Then Antoinette began to cry in a hopeless way.

"You don't understand," she said. "I'm not Germaine Ducrois—I'm Antoinette Ricci. It was my father, Giovanni Ricci, you shot. I sold you to the police out of revenge."

I nearly dropped her in my surprise.

"Antoinette Ricci? I remember you as a little girl. How you have altered!"

I set her down to listen for sounds of the pursuit. I had cut away from the main track, but expecting this, the police were working out in fan formation, I could hear them shouting to one another.

"But if you wanted the police to get me, whatever made you come out and warn me?" I demanded, thoroughly bewildered.

She did not answer for a moment, then she said, so quietly that I could scarcely hear her, "I found out that I loved you."

While we had been talking I was making a quick examination of her wounds. There were two and they were worse than I expected.

"*Chérie*," I said, "if I take you to the mountains with me you will get very poor nursing."

"Then leave me here," she answered quickly. "I shall be all right. The police will see to that. Yes, I shall have better care if I stay. Now go, André."

And so I went, leaving her lying there. I could already hear the nearest police tramping through the bush not fifty yards from where we lay. If Antoinette had felt that we could have got safely away to the mountains together, no promise of better nursing would have made her stay behind. I realize now that it was only her fear lest, trying to take her with me, I would be overtaken and killed by the police.

Poor Antoinette Ricci! She had paid a very heavy price for her attempted revenge and I bore her no ill will; rather I remembered the way she had thrown herself in between me and the young gendarme as he was about to fire upon me.

Wherever I went during those days the memory of Antoinette's sacrifice haunted me. And I could get no definite news of her. Some said that she had been removed to a hospital in Ajaccio, others that she was still in Coggia; yet another told me that she was at my parents' home being cared for by my mother. Some even said that she was dead.

The uncertainty worried me terribly. I did not blame her for wishing to bring about my death in return for the death of her father. I admired her for it. She was only living up to the law of the vendetta that demands a life for a life. If she were deserving of any blame it was because she had weakened at the last moment. But can you blame a woman for falling in love with you?

I have seen death too often in our troubled island to think much of it. But the thought of Antoinette lying dead for my sake affected me very deeply. I couldn't rest, for I could see her in my dreams. It was the first time that death had troubled me. When my comrades were killed I had naturally been sorry. But we spent our lives in such an atmosphere that death, when it came, meant little. For a while there was a gap: soon it was filled and one forgot. And when you killed a man it meant even less. It possibly seems a strange outlook on life to a Northerner, but killing a man meant very little more than killing an animal. Less even. I have grieved over the loss of a favorite mare; I have never felt moved to shed tears over the death of a gendarme.

But Antoinette Ricci's death, if she were dead, seemed different. I cannot explain it. It just did. It moved me more than anything that had ever happened. It made me careless of what might happen to me. If only I could know for certain, I would tell myself, I would be satisfied; but from nobody could I obtain any definite news of what had happened to her.

It was in this frame of mind that, some time later, I went down to my father's house near Coggia. I had heard several rumors that Antoinette had last been seen there. Possibly they were true. In any event my parents might know something of what had happened to her.

Since the last attempt at my capture I had lost touch with my spies or, no doubt, I could have obtained definite news from them. Possibly they had become frightened and were keeping out of my way in case they got into trouble with the police. I had been relying since then on odd scraps of information from the peasants who were still friendly. But the information one got from them was not always reliable, it lacked the authentic touch of my own paid spies.

My parents welcomed me as warmly as ever and begged me to have a meal. I was only too pleased to accept, for other than what I had been able to obtain in the more remote districts—and they were so poor that they had barely enough for themselves—I had scarcely eaten since the night Antoinette Ricci had been shot.

As soon as my parents' welcome was over I asked after Antoinette, and was deeply grieved to learn that she had died a couple of days after receiving the bullets meant for me.

We had scarcely begun our meal when there came a loud explosion just outside the house.

I leaped to my feet and seized my rifle, but my mother laid her hand on my arm.

"Let your father go to the door," she begged. "They will not harm him."

We waited tensely whilst his heavy steps crossed the hall. Then we heard the rattle of the bolts as he opened the door and called out:

"Who's there?"

"The police, M. Gavini," came the reply. "We know your son is in the house. Tell him to strip and come out into the open with his hands above his head."

My father came back into the room.

"You heard?" he asked.

I nodded.

"Then what are we going to do?"

I had already made up my mind. If it had been any other house I would have fought it out, though I knew that I had no chance. But, at the first sign of resistance, the house would be fired and my parents burnt alive.

"I shall surrender," I said, and going into the passage began to remove my clothes. They had once been so fine, those garments, my velvet coat and breeches, my silk shirt, my colored waistcoat, my tie. Now they were torn, dirty and bloodstained. One by one I laid them aside until I stood, in the darkness of that narrow hall, just as nature had made me. Only I held my stiletto in my hand.

I had a vague idea of leaping out and making a last stand. But somehow the spirit seemed to have gone out of me.

Antoinette Ricci may have relented in her attempt to betray: but in death she had succeeded. It was in search of news of her that I had come to this house when my usual caution warned me against it. And it was this new, odd sensation of fatality that had come with her death that now made me throw my stiletto aside and, with my hands raised above my head, step out to meet the police.

And so the last of the bandit chiefs of Corsica gave up his liberty.

A couple of *agents de police* leapt forward and clicked the handcuffs about my wrists, and with a coat thrown over my shoulders, I was hustled into a police car and conveyed to the barracks at Vico.

Later I was removed to Ajaccio gaol, where I still am. On my way to the gaol I was submitted to the indignity of being led through the streets instead of being driven in the police car. I suppose the authorities were so overjoyed at finally arresting me after so many bitter failures, that they wished to parade their success before the town.

The whole population, I should think, had turned out to watch the spectacle. They lined the streets, some hissing and booing, others silent. They were the townsfolk and had less sympathy with me than the peasantry who had known my help and protection for eleven years.

Since my arrest I had eaten practically nothing, and I felt weak and ill from the lack of food and the reaction after my surrender. As I was dragged along the cobbled streets I could scarcely stand. Several times I staggered; more than once I fell to my knees, only to be jerked to my feet again by my guards.

The men who lined the streets laughed.

"See!" they cried. "The brave Spada prays!"

Others called out that I had gone mad, that the great André Spada was a lunatic.

I cannot forget the torture of that procession through the streets of Ajaccio. It haunts me at nights. The jeering, grinning faces; the cries of derision; the abusive and cruel remarks.

But I shall remember, too, the voice of a woman in the crowd and the look of scorn she turned on the grinning apes of men about her.

"Once," she said, "there were men in Corsica who were men."

After that I cared little for the jeers and taunts.

I saw only the tears in the eyes of the women I passed and I felt the compassion that was in their hearts.

On June 8th I was brought up for trial on the charge of illegally carrying firearms.

In their attempt to crush the vendetta, the possession of firearms, otherwise than double-barreled shotguns, is an offence. I was found guilty and sentenced to two years' imprisonment and a fine of a thousand francs.

That was nothing, of course, but an excuse for holding me until the authorities have time to formulate their real charges against me.

I understand that the trial is to be in November, and there is talk of it being held, not in my native Corsica, but in France, probably Marseilles, where the authorities will have less to fear from the friends of the King of the Maquis.

And as I sit day after day in my cell in Ajaccio prison, knowing that the guillotine is hungering for my neck, I live again, in my memory, the days of my freedom. And it is the women I remember more than the men.

My thoughts turn but little to the many fights I have had with the police and rival bandits; rather I remember the loves that I have known.

I close my eyes and I can see a big orange moon shining through that creeper near Barcelona; I can see Mimi's eyes flashing tempestuously into mine; I can feel the warm blood from Antoinette Ricci's wounds on my hands; I can hear the soft voice of Antoinette Leca and see her tears when her child died.

If only he had lived. There would have been an heir to the "Kingdom of the Green Palace."

Afterword:

The Life and Death of a "Bandit of God," by Rob Couteau

There are at least two André Spadas. One is a charismatic raconteur, determined to convince the reader that he's an admirable Robin Hood: a heroic outlaw, stealing from those undeserving businessmen, and giving a percentage to the poor (the Corsican peasants, who serve as a spy network and who clearly lead a hardscrabble existence). Theft, in the form of extortion or the paying of tributes,[18] he calls "protection money." And he regards himself as an "honorable" man, even signing his income tax returns "Bandit of honor and of vengeance."[19]

The other Spada is a sociopath who doesn't hesitate to injure or kill innocent bystanders (for example, during raids on the postal service) as long as he can augment his power and increase his booty.

The autobiography is largely a chronicle of the first Spada, the charming psychopath, let's call him, but many of the journalists from this period are preoccupied with painting a more dire portrait: one centered round the sociopathic murderer and his sensational exploits. The only reason he doesn't steal from the poor, they say, is that the poor have nothing worth stealing.

One should also note that the first Spada doesn't always bother to camouflage the presence of the second Spada. How else account for the opening lines of this confession?

---

[18] "He considered the highway between Ajaccio and Sopigna his personal property [and] collected tribute from all travelers for years." "Happy as a Cuckoo," *Time* magazine, 18 March 1935, Time.com.

[19] "Spada on Trial Today," *Daily Herald* (London), 4 March 1935, p. 6.

> To have lived to the full, to have loved, to have fought,
> to have killed: that is a man's life. And even though the
> price be death, it would be cheap at that. No man has
> lived fully till he has loved deeply and often; no man
> has the right to the title of "Man" till he has fought and
> won; no man has tasted the fullest measure of power
> till he has killed.

But wherever one's loyalties as a reader lie, certain facts cannot be gainsaid. For example, innocent people were accidentally injured and killed; and many who were forced to pay "protection" suffered economic hardship, especially during the Great Depression.

Then there's that disturbing account of kidnap and torture. Even Spada himself admits that he crossed the line when, during a drunken frenzy, he horribly maimed Mimi Caviglioli's brother for refusing to betray Mimi, who had spurned Spada and run away. The lad, he tells us, was "barely more than a boy, a slight, clean-limbed youth." His resemblance to Mimi and his stubborn insolence fuels Spada's anger, which, in turn, propels him to drink excessively. Then we read those ominous words:

> Neat whisky on an empty stomach is liable to go to
> even the strongest head. I think as I sat there drinking I
> can have been hardly sane; jealousy and neat whisky
> are to blame for what I did that night.

The question of sanity foreshadows Spada's ultimate fate. But what immediately follows is even more extraordinary, because it's a confession of wrongdoing. Since sociopaths rarely make a public admission of regret – especially one involving harm to others – his words seem to leap from the page:

> Of what followed I have no very clear recollection, and
> I am glad, for it is something I want to forget…. I have

said that I have only one regret, and that was for what happened to Mimi's young brother. And that is the truth. When I have killed, and that has been often, it has been in fair fight or to avenge some wrong. This youth had no chance of defending himself and he, personally, had done me no wrong.

But elsewhere the "second Spada" will declare: "To regret is weak."

Despite claiming to kill only in a fair fight or for revenge, Spada makes no mention of those he murdered who just happened to be standing in the wrong place at the wrong time. Instead of making a habit of voicing remorse, he proudly boasts: "I have never regretted that impulse that made me an outlaw from society and the 'King of the Maquis.'" He was also known for the hubristic declaration: "I, Spada, am universal even before being Corsican ... I only know those who know me; others can suffer" – the ultimate narrow-minded view of a clannish reprobate lacking an elementary sense of humanity. Compare this to what happens when his predecessor, Nonce Romanetti, kills a police officer in a fair fight:

Then he went out; but first he stood a few moments staring down regretfully at the rash young officer's body.

He was like that, was Romanetti. Never a murderer, hardly a killer even, and even when he did kill it was in self-defense and with much subsequent regret.

To me it seemed a sign of weakness, this regret of his. When you kill a man in fair fight, when it is a question of his life or yours, what is there to regret?

If a man killed me in fair fight I would not expect him to weep over my dead body. Why, then, should I weep over his?

Poor Romanetti! In many ways he was a dreamer, an idealist, but there was no denying that, with it all, he was a very great leader and a brave man.

Or compare it to a scene in which Spada ambushes the gendarmes while they transport his friend across the mountains. Moments after he murders them, Spada reflects:

I had just killed two men, but oddly enough I felt quite calm. Drawing out a packet of cigarettes, I tossed one to Ferrari and lit another for myself.

"I suppose you realize," I asked him, "that we are now outlaws?"

Ferrari nodded.

"The police will never rest until they have sent us to the guillotine."

I sat down on a boulder and puffed slowly at my cigarette. It was like a dream, sitting there and smoking calmly when only a few minutes earlier I had killed two gendarmes. I felt no more excitement than I would if I had killed a couple of chickens for dinner.

Even in the final days of his life, during his court trial, it was pathological pride rather than modest remorse that dominated his spirit.

In any case, these are extreme acts, and therefore it's natural, on the part of the reader, to raise moral questions as the account unfolds. But Spada is a complex amalgam, not only of Good and Evil but also of contrary emotions and perceptions. These include compassion and kindness as well as those cold-blooded instincts that eclipse the humanity of those driven by abject criminality. But more importantly, beyond the idiosyncratic biography of a particular individual, it's through this chronicle that we gain entrée into a uniquely structured demimonde: an underworld constructed upon a rigid set of codes.

***

One of the primary questions to emerge from the dense scrub of the pine-covered maquis concerns the twining of free will and destiny. How is a man shaped by the cultural crucible into which he's born? As Spada himself recounts, in the late nineteenth- and early twentieth century, honor and vendetta were the twin gods round which the Corsican cosmos revolved. Defending one's honor through whatever means necessary – including extortion, kidnap, or murder ... such notions may seem antiquated to a politically correct generation, especially one programmed with knee-jerk reactions to anything that doesn't precisely align with its own predictable morality. But in the Corsica of Spada's time, the only thing that a man really possessed was his reputation, and the means to protect it frequently involved violence.

If we tinker with the vocabulary a bit, we can see that "honor" is not such a different thing from what is now referred to as "self-respect" or – that most wretched bromide – "self-empowerment." For Spada and the men of his generation, losing one's cool in the face of a gun barrel with its trigger primed and ready to fire was an alien notion ... precisely because they held so tightly to their self-esteem. But it was condensed into that simple term, *honor*. And as a Corsican proverb has it, *Ancu l'onore so castichi*: "Even upholding honor is a torment" – because of the obligation it entails. Remaining loyal to one's comrades, even if it results in a self-abnegating death, was a nonnegotiable value. As we can see from this account, after his friend is unjustly arrested by the gendarmes, Spada does what his culture has taught him to do: he attacks the officers in order to rescue his pal. That single act delivers him to the maquis – a veritable Underworld ruled by an even more ruthless set of gods than those in Greek myth. But one senses that, had it not been for this event, some other twist of fate would have brought Spada there, where he was destined to become the King of the Maquis. His "admirer," the English author Edith Halford Nelson, called him a "victim of destiny."[20] As Spada himself remarked to his brother: "We did not become bandits from choice; destiny pushed us into it."[21]

One should not gloss over this important point. To the extent that a bandit is born into "the life" – ineluctably imprisoned by it, even against his own better judgment or will – to that extent we can allow ourselves to empathize with his plight, even if he's a murderer.[22] For to live means to eat, and to eat means to kill. One slaughters either a fruit or a vegetable; a chicken or a duck; a man or a beast. The circumstances of birth determine what will be on the menu, but inevitably one kills. And without some degree of empathy, we cannot fully enter into our subject. The point is not to forgive, but to comprehend. Once again, context is everything.

---

[20] "Englishwoman's Amazing Love Letter to Corsican Bandit," *Manchester Evening News*, 21 November 1931, p. 5. During her first meeting with Spada, Edith Halford Nelson (née Thompson; 1878 – 1946) gave him a large signet ring, which he was wearing when he was captured. (See Lucia Molinelli-Cancellieri, *Spada, dernier bandit corse*, Paris: Julliard, 1986, p. 120.) Newsreels of Spada's trial include close-ups of the ring, glittering brightly on his finger. Nineteen years his senior, in the fall of 1931 Edith was fifty-three, while Spada was thirty-four. Her first encounter with the bandit (late April 1930) is described in a series of articles she published in the *Petit Marseillais*; and in "Adventure in Corsica with the Bandit Andre Spada," chapter twenty-three of her memoir, *Out of the Silence*, pp. 76-80. According to this chronicle, their relationship was platonic. Spada was interested in Edith's self-professed ability to foretell the future; he was also aware of her close association with the famous occultist known as "Cheiro." For more on Edith Nelson, see Appendix A and B (below).

[21] Stephen Wilson, *Feuding, Conflict and Banditry in Nineteenth-Century Corsica*, Cambridge, UK: Cambridge University Press, 2003, p. 341.

[22] Thanks to Robert De Sena, founder of Council for Unity, for this unique insight. See my interview with De Sena in Rob Couteau, *More Collected Couteau*, New York: Dominantstar, 2020, pp. 227-255.

If one can momentarily suspend judgment and just let go and enter into the tale, then there's bitter tragedy, comedy both light and dark, and an undercurrent of both excitement and horror. But let's not forget love. For as cold and monstrous as Spada could be, he was also driven by the need to submit himself to passion via the Wonder of Woman. Smitten by Eros, it's both a love of women and the love of a particular woman that gets him into trouble in the first place – and that finishes him off in the end.

***

Spada's disregard for the value of human life was eventually counterpointed by an obsession with religious ideation. But how did the devil come to emulate the angels? After so many dreary months of stealthily wandering through the icy mountains, narrowly escaping arrest while nearly starving to death, Spada eventually lost his mind. For the hunter had now turned into the hunted.

Evidence for this began to appear in the press. Spada had long enjoyed a reputation for taunting authorities and manipulating events by sending messages to local newspapers.[23] On 22 April 1932 he penned a letter, composed in a beautifully ornate calligraphy, to the editor of *L'Eveil d'Ajaccio*. The thought process and manner of expression evidenced in this missive, replete with loose associations, exhibits telltale signs of what is clinically termed "paranoid schizophrenia." But this label doesn't do justice to the rich symbolism resonating in such seemingly nonsensical phrasing. Consider, for example, the events lurking behind these words:

---

[23] Spada was one of the only bandit chiefs who was literate.

> If the good Lord forgave the leaders of the Voluntary
> Bandits, he would have doubly forgiven me, being a
> bandit by force to avenge the innocent.

This dovetails with what I remarked upon earlier: we can enter into the existential situation of those born into "the life" only when we realize that many of them had little choice but to become outlaws. The moment his friend was threatened by the gendarmes Spada leapt into action "to avenge the innocent," because he felt he had no other option. He was compelled to respond, driven as much by his deeply ingrained cultural values as by his fiery, impulsive temperament ... and by his loyalty and love for his friend. Then he became a "bandit by force" – acted upon by the innumerable elements that shape human destiny.

At first glance many would regard Spada's communiqué as mere babble. Yet, by probing a little deeper, we uncover a message rife with meaning despite being indecipherable to most psychiatric clinicians, who are trained to ignore the motifs encoded within such "psychotic" thought forms. Until recently, to explore the intricacies of a schizophrenic's hallucination was regarded as "feeding into his delusional system" – a psychiatric taboo. But if God was ever in the details, he would surely be lurking there. Thus, when Spada makes his appeal "for the innocents who are paying for the guilty," we read this in a new, more meaningful light.

> From today onwards, I declare war on injustice and all
> those whom I feel may assist it in its work. In the name
> of Our Lord Jesus Christ, be prepared[,] because my
> weapon is ready wherever I encounter them, armed or
> not; their blood will flow on the ground like the tears
> of innocents that have flowed in prison.

Spada's pledge to protect the innocent and his threat to destroy their persecutors (the dastardly gendarmes!) reads like an autobiographical reference. One wonders: Is he harkening back to his own lost innocence, now quashed and irretrievable but echoing with everlasting reverberation, as if from the sepulchral depths of a mausoleum?

Near the bottom of the final page he inscribes a large "Holy Cross": an icon not only of Christianity but also a symbol that autonomously manifests during moments of severe psychic stress. Both the Western cross and the Eastern mandala are expressions of an inner compass: a quaternity radiating from a center, which attempts to instill psychological reorientation and emotional well-being.

In sum, such invocations tell us much about the fugitive's fragile mental state, thirteen months before his capture.

***

In the spring of 1933, audiences were entertained by a *British Movietone* newsreel, "Notorious Bandit Gives Himself Up," which portrays the rude setting of Spada's arrest. The film opens with an exterior view of his parents' humble, whitewashed dwelling. Then our gaze focuses on several uniformed gendarmes, who pace around the tiny abode in Coggia. There, on 29 May 1933, a barefoot, nearly naked Spada – an oversized crucifix dangling from his neck – emerged at daybreak.[24] With a

---

[24] The charismatic photogenic bandit was no stranger to the cinema. On 24 February 1931, Spada met with a Pathé Cinema film crew deep within the Maquis, about thirty-seven miles from Ajaccio. In exchange for a hefty sum of cash, he agreed to be interviewed by the journalists Harry Grey and Christine Hubert. ("Harry Grey" was the pseudonym of Herschel Goldberg, an American born in the Ukraine.) The documentary was widely distributed to both French and international cinemas. (A copy is stored at the Regional Film Archive in Porto-Vecchio, a town on the southeastern coast of Corsica.)

wobbly gait he ambled into the awaiting arms of the police, who swiftly cuffed his wrists.[25] According to an Associated Press dispatch, he was gaunt and confused. "His once burly figure has shrunk to a scant 110 pounds," and he was wearing "little else" but a "crown of flowers." Others describe it as a "crown of thorns." A bubbly *Movietone* voice-over proclaims that the bandit surrendered "in a fit of religious fervor, having recently become a prey to a conversion psychosis."

Several days later, on 2 June 1933, Spada posed for a mug shot. Bearing the same sort of savage beauty that one encounters in the façade of a rocky promontory or a well-worn, glistening conch shell, Spada's physiognomy appears to be polished by elemental forces such as wind or rain. His dilating pupils burn with the same intensity as Picasso's jet-black Mediterranean orbs; yet, unlike the joy that often twinkled in the artist's eyes, Spada's gaze is troubled, as if focused upon the *horror vacui*. The image calls to mind a remark he made fifteen months earlier, in a letter to a female companion: "Again there came to me the sensation of the hunted animal for whom there is nothing but the fight to the death."[26]

Initially charged with weapons possession, he will eventually be tried for committing over a dozen murders.

According to another journalist, Spada's going rate was "£500 for a two-hour newsreel, and £140 for a ten-minute broadcast." See *Smith's Weekly* (Sydney, Australia), 13 April 1935, p. 17. Biographer Lucia Molinelli-Cancellieri reports: "Fascinated by Spada's strange personality, Christine Hubert became his mistress." Lucia Molinelli-Cancellieri's *Spada, dernier bandit corse*, p. 120. (My translation.)

[25] "In May 1933, peasants going to mass in the village of Coggia found a hoarse, half-crazed man shouting 'What have I done?' in front of the church door. A crown of thorns was in his hair and a heavy wooden cross hung from his neck. It was André Spada." "Happy as a Cuckoo," *Time* magazine, 18 March 1935, Time.com.

[26] See "Corsican Outlaw Barely Gets Away, Chased From Lair to Lair Until His Nerves Become Shaky," *Chattanooga Daily Times*, 28 February 1932, p. 13.

***

It's perhaps fitting that Spada returned to his parents' home for sustenance and that he was captured there after first appearing at the village church. I say this because the mafia mentality is often synonymous with that of the *puer aeternus*: the eternal youth who refuses to fully mature and who believes that it's his *right* to remain, metaphorically speaking, at the mother's breast. This negative aspect of the mother / son archetype – with its uncut umbilical cord – is deeply ingrained in the Mediterranean culture, whose voluptuous seduction may be so profound that the notion of working for a living becomes an anathema.[27] Indeed, more than once in this account, Spada refers to daily labor as if it's an embarrassment:

> I was not fond of work, particularly under another man's direction.

> The War was over. Once again I was returned to my beloved Corsica and had settled at my parents' house in Lopigna. As one must work to live, even in Corsica, unless one is a rich man or a bandit, I went back to my old occupation, that of a forester.

> Barcelona is a busy city and there is generally work to be found there for a strong young man. Yes, I intended to work.

Whatever a fellow can do to avoid it – including rape, pillage, or plunder – is viewed as justifiable if it removes the yolk of human bondage. Just as a child expects a free meal, the "career"

---

[27] For a cinematic treatment of this theme, see Federico Fellini's *I Vitelloni* (1953).

criminal feels that it's his right to take without paying a price. He's *entitled* to steal, but he remains under no obligation to contribute value to society.

Thus, when he has nowhere else to go, Spada returns to the shelter of the maternal domicile[28] and to the hallowed haunches of the Great Mother Church. The child-man, suffering from "arrested development," is then, quite literally, placed under arrest.

***

Photos of the imprisoned Spada stand in vivid contrast to his initial mug shot; for they portray a man with a beatific smile, his eyes merrily shining. No doubt, his religious conversion experience was authentic, but neither can there be any doubt that, by the end, he had drifted into psychosis.[29] Throughout his trial, much to the chagrin of his lawyers, Spada freely bestowed self-incriminating remarks upon the prosecution, even during a crucial juncture in which his defense team had been working to exonerate him of a major crime. In this regard, my favorite exchange is the following, which is hard to beat for pure black humor. When a judge asks, "How many men did you kill?" Spada replies

> "I don't remember exactly, but you can count the notches I cut into the butt of my rifle."

---

[28] Earlier in his account Spada writes: "As the winter receded and spring drew on, this 'homesickness' ... grew more intense. Finally, it became so strong that I decided to risk capture and spend Easter with my parents."

[29] Spada's illiterate father exhibited far more insight than the psychiatric "experts" when he succinctly concluded: "My son is not crazy, but it is his existence in the maquis that puts him in this state." The implication is that Spada wasn't born crazy but that his lifestyle had driven him to madness. See Lucia Molinelli-Cancellieri, *Spada, dernier bandit corse*, p. 202.

The judge ordered a court attendant to count the notches in the bandit's rifle, which had been introduced in court among the legal pieces of evidence.

"Twenty-eight, your honor," said the court attendant after a while.

"So you killed twenty-eight men?" said the judge, turning to the bandit. "Fathers of families, sons of ..." His honor did not finish speaking before Spada interrupted: "Heavens, no; that's only one rifle. I have three more guns hidden somewhere."[30]

The egomaniacal "King" who required constant affirmation – whether it be derived from the power he exerted over others, or from the accrual of illicit riches, or from the beautiful fawning women who fell under his sway – would have been crushed if forced to consciously confront the dire reality of his new circumstances: locked up in gaol and supervised like an animal in a cage. Instead, honor remained intact because God himself was now listening to Spada's every word as the prisoner's gaze was cast heavenward.

When a prosecutor concluded his remarks by proclaiming: "You have played and lost! Now, pay up!," Spada grinned and nodded emphatically, his eyes glazed and shiny, his smile ever more radiant. One account has him replying, "God has decided so." Asked about his crimes, he exclaimed: "You speak of blood? I am responsible – period!"[31]

Apparently the "Bandit of God" was looking forward to meeting his maker. Perhaps he'd envisioned his arrival in heaven as an encounter between royal highnesses, and execution by guillotine was merely the vehicle of transportation. (As he informed the magistrate: "I have only one master, and He alone

---

[30] *Star Weekly* (Toronto), 20 April 1935, p. 37.

[31] Jacques Simon Timotei, "Les Bandits Corses: André Spada," Corsicamea.fr. My translation.

will judge me.")[32] Moments before his execution, when an officiating priest muttered the word "Courage," Spada retorted: "I'm not afraid. I've settled my accounts with God – that's all that matters. The day I entered prison I approached Christ. I am sure he has pardoned me."[33] "I am killed only as an agent of heaven. If heaven had not ordered me to surrender, hundreds more would have died."[34] And lady-killer that he was, dozens more would have had their hearts broken.

Maybe there's a place in the next world for a man in possession of such unusual skills but who could find no suitable earthly role that didn't involve the spilling of blood. Since no one has ever heard of *working* in heaven, Spada was probably looking forward to an eternal life of leisure. Perhaps it was for this reason that he strolled so "casually" to the guillotine."[35]

***

According to various psychological studies, only gainful employment can serve as an antidote to the *puer* complex. Although this may sound like a simplistic solution, nothing could be closer to the truth; for only through labor can we give birth to something meaningful. Hence the proviso *gainful*, which connotes not only profitable to the pocketbook but also fulfilling to the spirit. Theft is a pilfering of another man's labor, so this results in a barren harvest: for one's innate talent, whatever it is, will never be cultivated or grow to fruition. In this sense, the criminal betrays himself. Indeed, as exciting as

---

[32] "Bandit King Faces His Trial," *Liverpool Echo*, 4 March 1935, p. 7.
[33] "Guillotine Ends Career of Bandit," *Rome Daily Sentinel* (Rome, New York), 22 June 1935, p. 1.
[34] "Stoic Brigand Warns World From Guillotine," *Knoxville Journal*, 22 June 1935, p. 1.
[35] "Corsican Bandit King Dies on Guillotine," *Philadelphia Inquirer*, 22 June 1935, p. 3.

the Spada tale is, it also highlights the banality of the entire criminal enterprise: its childishness; its petty squabbles; its empty heroics.

In this regard, some etymological digging leads to some unexpected nuggets. For example, take the word *extortion*. Merriam-Webster dictionary informs us that it doesn't apply only to protection money: "To extort is literally to wrench something out of someone." (Recall the kidnapped Caviglioli, whose torture results in the wrenching out of the young man's soul.) The etymological chain is linked thus: "Latin *extortus*, past participle of *extorquēre*, to wrench out, extort, from *ex- torquēre*, to twist — more at *torture*, entry 1."

Now let's see where *torture* leads us: "From Late Latin *tortura*, from Latin *tortus*, past participle of *torquēre*, to twist. Probably akin to Old High German *drāhsil*, turner; Greek *atraktos*, spindle." Thus the twisted impulses lurking behind both *torture* and *extortion* share the same root.

Next we examine the term for hard work, *travail* ("Work especially of a painful or laborious nature: toil") – the very thing most abhorred by Spada. "Etymologists are pretty certain that *travail* comes from *trepalium*, the Late Latin name of an instrument of torture."

Instead of submitting themselves to the "torture" of work, Spada and his ilk inverted the normal pattern and engaged in the "work" of torture, rendered through physical or economic means. Spada even qualifies the nature of his particular brand of toil. Reflecting on his life, which he compares to "a wonderful book," he says

> I can look back upon my life as a reader can look back upon a book whose last chapter has been reached and which yet lies open upon his knee. Its pages are written in blood and bespattered with the sweat of toil: but not the toil that most men know, the axe, the

plough, the anvil, the bench. My toil has been an unsleeping alertness, as of a wild animal, always on the watch for its hunters, ever ready to pounce upon its prey, never relinquishing its tension lest some false move may betray its whereabouts and the crack of a gun and the searing heat of a bullet shall end its days.

But there's another side to all this: one that can never be framed by mere psychologizing. While the media outlets focused on Spada's misdeeds, they paid little heed to the State-sponsored torture meted out by French colonialists, with their brutal repression of human rights. It was this abysmal behavior that triggered the resistance of the Corsican underworld: the men known as the Maquis or *Maquisards*, who refused to bow to those Cartesian conquerors who marched with ice water in their veins.

The Maquis had no need to engrave *Liberté, Égalité, Fraternité* upon the cold granite of municipal buildings. Instead of a hollow pretense of liberty, equality, and fraternity they lived the very thing those words falsely proclaimed. And besides, they possessed other objects, engraved with more passionate terms, that preserved their sacred truths. As the Corsican artist Jules Mondoloni recently informed me:

> I understand this fascination for the "honest" bandit, Spada. You ask a Corsican what he thinks of it! The taste for revenge is in our genes. Knives are sold for tourists, called "Vendetta," on which the phrase is engraved: *Che la mia ferita sia mortale* (May my wound be mortal) or "Vendetta Corsa." Everyone had one in their pocket. A taste that dates, I believe, from the occupation of the island by the Bank (or Republic) of Geneva. The Corsicans took the law into their own hands, because the Genoese justice only protected the colonizing lords. But no doubt the Corsican also hates

injustice. The *Maquisards* of the war against fascism acted in this direction and for the sacrosanct freedom, our characteristic trait. I myself grew up with these stories about the lives of honor, bandits, highwaymen, or political struggles.

The word for knife is *Cultella* or *Culteddu* in my region in the south. Your name would be honored on my island![36]

This undercurrent of political struggle[37] entices the reader to root for the honorable bandits, especially when, despite being hunted like rats, they manage to pick off a few of their pursuers. Suddenly we are there with Spada, huddled beside the entrance of the cave at midnight, rolling a boulder down the rocky cliff in order to trick the gendarmes, who pivot to the left as we jettison down the precipice to the right.

As we sprint away, our footfalls masked by the roar of the river, we head upstream and then cut across to the sheltering undergrowth of the maquis. We made it; we escaped; and, once again, we have "lived to the full."

Perhaps Spada was right to say that, in exchange for such adventure, death is a small price to pay.

***

Spada lost his head to Madame la Guillotine on 21 June 1935. Moments before his death he matter-of-factly remarked, "It was never courage that I lacked." When offered the traditional glass of rum and a cigarette, he waved them aside. "I never smoked

---

[36] In French, *couteau* means knife.

[37] In his autobiography Spada writes: "The world, they say, is turning to Socialism, to the helping of the poor from the rich man's pocket. If that is so then not only was I King of the Maquis but King of Socialism, for that is how we lived, we bandits, helping the poor at the unwilling rich man's expense."

or drank in my life! Why should I begin now? I don't need a drink to help me die."[38]

The journalistic accounts of his exploits, capture, and death vary widely: some have him surrendering at his parents' home, some at the village church, others at an isolated cabin with a lover. But one thing they all agree upon is that André "Spada" Gavini met his fate calmly and bravely. According to one account, while his neck rested on the block, his final words were: "I am going straight to paradise, because I've been touched with divine grace."

He was buried in an anonymous grave in the old cemetery of Porette, in Bastia.

---

[38] See "Death of Spada," *Time* magazine, 1 July 1935, Time.com; and "Guillotine Ends Career of Bandit," *Rome Daily Sentinel* (Rome, New York), 22 June 1935, p. 1.

"I sought refuge in the Maquis."

Timeline

13 February 1897. Birth of André to Mr. Gavini and Anna-Maria Berti in Ajaccio, Corsica. One of nine children, he later changes his surname to "Spada," which means "sword."

[Age 12] 1909. Lopigna, Corsica. Works with his father as a lumberjack and charcoal burner, a profession known for its arduous labor. He later informs the journalist Christine Hubert: "My father was a charcoal burner. If there's a tough job, it is certainly that one. We leave the women and children at home and go far away, into the maquis, with four or five companions, on behalf of a charcoal contractor. I've done this job; I know it well. We go up there, far away from everything, to the area destined to be turned into charcoal. We don't look at the landscape, no. We are not there for that. With great strokes of the axe, we fell a few trees, and then immediately we get to work. The pay is made, so to speak, by the piece, per quintal. So we have to chop wood and hurry to cook it so that it produces a lot of charcoal. We swing the axe at dawn and only stop when the sun has set. Sometimes, to earn more, we get up several hours before daybreak and work by moonlight."

[Age 20] 1917. Enlists in the artillery, which enables him to acquire French nationality.

[Age 22] 1919. Sentenced for desertion during wartime. Subsequently amnestied and then allowed to reenlist, to fight in Syria.

[Age 24] May 1921. Returns to Corsica.

[Age 25] 8 October 1922. While attending a festival in Sari d'Orcino, Spada's childhood friend Antoine Rutili is wrongfully detained for an attack on an Italian sailor. Spada fires at the gendarmes, rescues Rutili, then goes into hiding. One gendarme is wounded, the other is killed. Days later, the man who actually attacked the sailor, Jean-Dominique Rubrini, surrenders to authorities.

[Age 26] 4 January 1924. Rutili is arrested and accused of murder. At first he receives a death sentence. His capture has a profound effect upon Spada, who sinks into depression. Rutili spends twenty-seven years in a brutal penal colony on the Salvation Islands, but he's finally granted a pardon.

[Age 28] 11 July 1925. With a price on his head, Spada is sentenced to death in absentia.

[Age 28] 9 November 1925. Spada murders Jacques Giocundi's sister (age twenty-two) and her elderly uncle, mistaking them for Marie ("Mimi") Caviglioli and her lover.

[Age 29] 25 April 1926. Spada's mentor Nonce Romanetti dies in a shoot-out with police in the mountains. This further aggravates Spada's melancholy. Overwhelmed by sorrow, he begins to commune with God.

[Age 29] 23 December 1926. To bolster his demands for being paid a tribute, Spada attacks a postal coach operating between Ajaccio and Lopigna. He injures the driver, Fanchi Delmo, and two of the twelve passengers.

[Age 33] 20 April 1930. Spada's brother Bastien fires three bullets into his enemy Jean-Ange Paoli. Four days later, after

Paoli dies in a hospital, Bastien slips into the maquis and joins Spada.

[Age 33] Late April 1930. Spada is interviewed by the occultist Edith Halford Nelson.

[Age 33] 18 May 1930. At first, Spada fails to obtain a new concession for the postal delivery service. In retaliation, his gang attacks the coach, killing a conductor and two gendarmes and seriously wounding a passenger. The van is then set on fire. Bastien kills one of the gendarmes just as he's about to fire at Spada, thus saving his brother's life. "It is thought that Spada desired only to frighten the driver and conductor as a warning that he intended to remain master of the line, but three gendarmes were travelling in the bus in an ordinary capacity, and Spada, imagining that they had come to capture him, at once opened fire, killing two of the gendarmes and the conductor." See "André Spada Executed," *The Advertiser* (Adelaide, Australia), 24 June 1935, p. 16.

[Age 34] 24 February 1931. Spada is interviewed by the journalists Harry Grey and Christine Hubert and proclaims himself "King of the Green Palace." The film is widely distributed in movie theaters. Fascinated by Spada, Christine becomes his mistress.

[Age 34] 8 November 1931. A French expeditionary force led by General Fournier is sent to Corsica to root out Spada and the bandits. The contingent is composed of tanks, planes, mountain artillery, a cannon, explosives, armored cars, field kitchens, and about 1,400 troops. But the expedition fails to capture Spada and is eventually withdrawn. It's later replaced by a police campaign, which succeeds in forcing

Spada out of his hideaway and driving him across the island.

[Age 34] 12 November 1931. A headline in the *Paterson Morning Call* (Paterson, New Jersey) reveals the military's strategy: "French Troops Hope To Starve Corsican Brigands Into Submission." A subheading declares: "One Wing of 'Army' Concentrating in Hunt for André Spada, Called Most Desperate of All Criminal Leaders on the Island." The article adds that Spada is currently "in the mountains near Punta, where he has established his bases."

[Age 34] 13 November 1931. The *Derby Daily Telegraph* (Derby, England) features a headline, "Eight Warships to Beat a Few Bandits," with the lead: "Two cruisers, six torpedo boats, strong naval and army patrols" [vs.] "André Spada, the walking arsenal, bandit leader, and his nephew. These are the opposing forces in Ajaccio, Corsica, which the French government hopes to clear of bandits – when they are caught." The article adds: "The warships were sent from the first French Mediterranean Squadron at Toulon … In addition to a small arsenal which he carries on his person, Spada is said to carry poison ready for instant use." Two French battleships, the *Lorraine* and the *Jean Bart*, participate in a naval blockade that surrounds the island, to prevent the bandits from escaping.

[Age 34] November 1931. Spada is forced out of his estate in Punta; dozens of his associates are arrested.

[Age 34] 23 November 1931. Under the heading "Corsican Bandits Hard Pressed," *The News* (Adelaide, Australia) reports: "22 November: André Spada and his brother, bandit leaders, are being hard pressed. They are half starved, and last night they entered a peasant's hut and demanded food. André Spada fell to the floor in a faint, but later recovered. They disappeared into the bush before the arrival of gendarmes. In a determined effort to wipe out the powerful bandits from Corsica an expeditionary force of 600 special police from France has raided their strongholds. Already 73 arrests have occurred. The police now are endeavoring to track down the remaining four or five leaders, including the notorious André Spada."

[Age 35] 28 February 1932. The *Chattanooga Daily Times* publishes a letter written by Spada that has fallen into the possession of the police. Addressing a female companion, Spada describes three close calls with pursuers, who come within inches of his hiding place on Christmas Eve. He concludes "Again there came to me the sensation of the hunted animal for whom there is nothing but the fight to the death." (See "Corsican Outlaw Barely Gets Away, Chased From Lair to Lair Until His Nerves Become Shaky.")

[Age 35] 7 March 1932. London's *Daily Herald* features a front-page article: "'Herald' Talk With Hunted Bandit. Spada Tells Why He Will Never Be Caught." During a secretly arranged meeting in the maquis, Spada informs a journalist: "I have been forced to live my life as I do through a vengeance of honor."

[Age 35] 22 April 1932. Spada's precarious mental state, which exhibits signs of psychosis, is revealed in a letter sent to *L'Eveil d'Ajaccio*. He declares "war on injustice and all those whom I feel may assist it in its work."

[Age 35] 18 May 1932. Under the heading "In Petticoats, Bandit Chief," *The World's News* (Sydney, Australia) reports that

Spada may have escaped detection while disguised as a woman. "Corsica's most notorious bandit, who eluded the police during their campaign to clean up the island last November, is being sought in the disguise of an elderly woman with pinched face and spectacles." "In this disguise, it is suggested, the bandit passed unnoticed through the police lines to his present place of safety."

[Age 35] 1 June 1932. After sheltering at his parents' house in Coggia, Bastien decides to surrender. His parents escort him to the public prosecutor's office in Ajaccio. A bounty of 100,000 francs is offered for Spada's head, but no one betrays him. Bastien informs his parents that Spada is deeply engrossed in his religious mania, which has driven a wedge between the brothers.

[Age 35] 5 July 1932. Spada sends a letter to the press that includes the passage: "Notice to all and to the grace of God, Spada André, bandit of honor and vengeance, but not a policeman, rather death a hundred thousand times than dishonor once. Here I am ready for peace and war, so I am ready for anything. God first and then I wish everyone what their heart desires." Some regard this as additional evidence of his mounting religiosity and deteriorating mental state.

[Age 35] 29 July 1932. In a dispatch from Nice, the *Bismarck Tribune* (Bismarck, North Dakota) reports: "André Spada, Corsican outlaw styled the 'overlord of the bush,' is defiant. He sent letters to newspapers on the Riviera challenging the French government to come into the maquis and get him. He said 100,000 Gardes Mobile couldn't catch him."

[Age 36] 22 February 1933. Bastia's Assize Court sentences Bastien to five years in prison and ten years of banishment.

[Age 36] 29 May 1933. After avoiding capture for eighteen months – barefoot, unarmed, and donning a large, roughly hewn crucifix – Spada surrenders to police at his parent's house. He's then incarcerated at the Ajaccio prison. Exhibiting signs of psychological decompensation, he's transported to Marseilles for psychiatric evaluation. But the psychiatric "experts" file a nonsensical report, filled with mistakes and inconsistencies, which concludes that the prisoner is feigning madness. One cannot help but suspect that these functionaries are merely doing the bidding of the State, which clearly wants to set an example.

[Age 36] 8 June 1933. In a preliminary trial, the Correctional Court of Ajaccio sentences Spada to two years imprisonment and fines him 1,000 francs for illegal possession of firearms.

[Age 36] 10 June 1933. Spada's *Mes mémoires*, compiled by Harry Grey and Christine Hubert, is published by Éditions Jules Tallandier, in Paris.

[Age 36] 17 November 1933. The *Daily Mirror* (London) features a brief piece titled "Happy in Gaol": "André Spada, the notorious Corsican bandit, who is serving a sentence of two years imprisonment, is so happy in gaol that he doesn't want anything else. He has refused a sum of money offered to him by a journalist who is writing a book of travel, in which André Spada figures largely. Heading his letter, 'House of Detention,' his reply reads as follows: 'I give you full permission to do as you wish in regard to the book of which you speak. As for me I personally do not want anything. I have all I want.'"

[Age 36] 7 December 1933. Spada pleads guilty to charges of "suspending a public service." (After gaining control of the Vico-Ajaccio postal service, Spada had suspended deliveries for a month.) Sentenced to five years imprisonment, he will later be tried for the murder of the two gendarmes who were riding on the coach.

[Age 37] 10 April 1934. Spada goes on a hunger strike at the Chave prison in Marseilles, where he's undergoing psychiatric evaluation.

[Age 37] January 1935. *Spada the Bandit* is published by Grayson and Grayson in London. The autobiography is edited by Robert Darrell, "From material supplied by André Spada." A Welsh businessman and writer who contributed to the *Herald of Wales*, "Darrell" is the pseudonym of H. Lesley Thomas, of Caswell, Swansea, Wales.

[Age 37] 29 January 1935. Confined at Sainte-Claire prison in Bastia.

[Age 38] 4 March 1935. Spada's court trial is held in a small opera house in Bastia and is filmed by *British Movietone*. His behavior alternates between profound indifference and witty theatrical repartee. He refuses to divulge the names of the many women in his life, but he confesses to murders that the prosecution isn't even aware of.

[Age 38] 6 March 1935. Found guilty of four murders, he is sentenced to death.

[Age 38] 20 June 1935. Spada is denied presidential clemency on the same day that an executioner arrives from Paris, along with a portable guillotine.

[Age 38] 21 June 1935. After playing cards with prison guards until midnight, Spada is executed in the courtyard at dawn. The *guillotineur* was as famous as Spada. For over four decades, Anatole Deibler (aka "Monsieur de Paris") conducted 401 executions, always dressed in an impeccable frock coat, derby, and white gloves. His one wish had been to retire to his villa in Saint-Cloud, to play with his turtles and tend to his prize roses, which he cultivated for a perfumery business. But instead, on 2 February 1939 Deibler died from pulmonary congestion while descending the stairs of a subway entrance, heading toward his next grisly assignment. Newspapers report that Deibler's assistants "anxiously awaited" him at Gare Montparnasse, while the portable guillotine (commonly referred to as "Madame de Paris" or "The Widow") was safely tucked away on the train.

Reviews of *Spada the Bandit*

— *Manchester Evening News*, 26 January 1935, p. 3.

— *Liverpool Daily Post*, 29 January 1935, p. 7.

— *Western Mail* (Cardiff, South Glamorgan, Wales), 31 January 1935, p. 10.

— *The Observer* (London), 5 May 1935, p. 7.

Appendix A:
Newspaper Articles About Spada

"Famous Bandit Shot Dead. Evaded Capture for 18 years. A Picturesque Corsican," *Liverpool Post and Mercury*, **27 April 1926, p. 8**

Paris, Monday. All the romance and legend of the most famous banditti of Corsica is recalled in the news that Nonce Romanetti has been ambushed and shot by gendarmes near Ajaccio.

For eighteen years Romanetti, the most notorious bandit of modern times, had defied all efforts to capture him, although, strange to say, he mingled a good deal in public life during that time. Well-known people visiting Corsica were often received by him in some secret place, and they ate and drank of the best in Corsica at his table.

Interviewed and Filmed.

He was interviewed, and his portrait appeared frequently in many newspapers. He had earned the name of the "Gentleman Bandit," for he was the hero of many a worthy incident. When a postal aeroplane between the South of France and Ajaccio fell near Alata in 1921, Romanetti was the first to help the passengers and to inform the authorities.

Periodically he appeared in the largest hotels in Corsica, and dined and drank nobly, and even joined in dancing. It is even stated that during the visit to the island of M. Millerand, when the latter was president of the Republic, Romanetti was among the mayors and prominent people who welcomed him.

His influence was shown by the fact that candidates in elections knew the value of having him on their side. His horses ran in several local races, the judges being generally warned beforehand which was to win. He was filmed in one of his safest retreats, the locality being surrounded by his own bodyguard, who, when danger threatened, kept guard over him, guns in hand, day and night.

His First Crime.

Romanetti began life as a butcher, and it was a shortage of meat at the local fete that led to his first crime. Details of the incident are lost in the past, but apparently he stole a bullock, intending to pay for it later. The farmer to whom the animal belonged laid a trap for Romanetti in order to betray him to the police. Romanetti escaped, but said to a friend: "Tell the farmer he will not hear the bullet that kills him." So the farmer paid the penalty, and Romanetti took to the marshes.

Three times he has been sentenced to death in his absence. Once he killed another bandit who had not played the game, and he shot two gendarmes who tried to capture him. Romanetti was a rich man, and gave bountifully to necessitous people in the island.

Details of his death show that he was killed near a famous house which he occupied, and which was built on a narrow rock promontory on the north coast of the island. Apparently he had recently suspected some of his followers, and he lived practically alone. The gendarmes knew that every morning he went to survey the work of building a huge cellar for the wine from the vineyard which he had created near this spot.

The Fatal Ambush.

On Sunday morning he was proceeding on horseback along the deserted rocky road leading to the vineyard with his faithful dog in front. Suddenly the dog began to bark. Romanetti adopted a defensive attitude just as he was being surrounded by gendarmes beyond the rock. Romanetti replied by firing at them, and they fired in return, bringing him from his horse. He swept the whole district with shot from a gun and a revolver before he died, shot through the abdomen.

"Bandit's Warning," *North Mail and Newcastle Daily Chronicle* (Newcastle upon Tyne, England), 3 September 1927, p. 6

André Spada has issued a manifesto that concerns ourselves – or as many of us as have ambitions to go touring in Corsica. André follows the calling of bandits, and as his father and grandfather and all his ancestors were members of the same profession he has a certain natural pride in the family practice. He says that he has nothing special against gendarmes; they are the constitutional opposition, so to speak. But he warns English tourists to keep off his beat, especially any who are disposed to show an undue desire to pry into his affairs, or to report what they have seen to the gendarmes. André does not want to be unpleasant, but – !

"Brigand Chief. Englishwoman Admirer of Spada. Strange Letter Found," *Birmingham Evening News* (Birmingham, West Midlands, England), 14 November 1931, p. 6

Among the documents found by the police at the home of André Spada, the hunted bandit chief in Corsica, is (says Reuter) a remarkable letter, in broken French, believed to have been written by an Englishwoman who spent a holiday in Corsica last year. It is addressed to "His Majesty the King of the Maquis" – the maquis is the dense undergrowth in Corsica – and runs: –

> Dear Mr. Spada, – In Corsica I am under the influence of a wonderful day spent with my friends and you. I write to thank you for your charming welcome, and for the royal banquet at which I was perhaps too overcome to do it justice.
>
> You will perhaps not be surprised to know that on leaving you I treasure in my heart the great desire to see the man who has so deeply impressed me with his smiling courage in face of an unjust and pitiless fate, and who by his own strength of will has dominated and forged his life anew.
>
> I live in this hope, and at your call I will come alone and fearless. In the meantime I think of you and every day pray to the Blessed Virgin.[39]

The Exchange correspondent at Ajaccio says the letter is signed "Edith."

So far there have been 96 arrests in the "war" against the bandits, but the ringleaders are still free.

---

[39] What the Blessed Virgin might have to do with Spada is anyone's guess.

Ring Round Forest

According to the correspondent of the "Daily Telegraph," the police and the mobile guards are digging themselves in with a thoroughness indicating that some of them at least feel that they will be stationed in the island for many weeks to come.

Spada's house at La Punta has been adopted as a permanent outpost. It stands on a windswept mountain known as "The Ridge of Death," and is a regular fortress, with walls at some points three feet thick. Loopholes for rifles or machine guns are pierced in them.

Spada, most dangerous of all the bandits, is believed to be hiding in a forest not far away, the Cruzzini Forest.

On all the ridges round this forest guards have been installed with machine guns. If Spada and the men, including his brother, who are believed to be with him, show themselves, their chances of breaking through the barrage are exceedingly small.

The police investigations have led to the discovery of some extraordinary facts about these outlaws. Recently a woman entered a shop in Ajaccio and selected lengths of silk to the value of £10. When she was asked to whom the bill should be sent she replied: "Oh, I am the mistress of the bandit Spada. You can send the bill to him." Naturally, that bill was never sent.

"Englishwoman's Amazing Love Letter to Corsican Bandit. Fascinated Woman's Bandit King. Love for Outlaw Revealed in Letter. Spada's English Captive," *Manchester Evening News*, 21 November 1931, p. 5

Ajaccio, Saturday. *"Bandit of honor, victim of destiny, sword of the maquis, bandit king."* Thus begins another extraordinary love letter addressed by an Englishwoman to the bandit André Spada, which has just come to light.

The letter, which is signed "Edith," is a kind of rapturous idyll, and continues as follows:

"He is my son. At night I hide him in my perfumed bosom close to my heart. I am his slave, his willing slave.

'"I cool his fevered brow and slake his thirst. Mine is the song that soothes hiss tortured brain.

"All nature loves the son of the maquis. Here in his palace green his will is law. Beware who disobeys! Beware who enters here with other thoughts than friendship! Death lurks in ambush for his enemies.

"When Spada is no more the forest, wrapped in gloom, will mourn him; the perfumed maquis will lie silent and desolate, bereft of song.

"Bandit of honor, victim of destiny, long may the maquis claim her bandit son."

André Spada, to whom this passionate outburst is addressed, is not only a desperate bandit but also breaker of feminine hearts, and his exploits with the fair sex have been numerous.

WOMEN FASCINATED

Young and strong, known as the "King of the Palais Vert" – the local name for the maquis – he has fascinated all who have come into contact with him.

Besides his two Corsican mistresses, he has captured the fancy of many foreign women tourists.

One of Corsica's most renowned bandits is a woman with the poetic name of Stellina de Foccicchia – "little star of Foccicchia." For years she has dominated the district after which she is named.

Stellina commenced her career at the age of 13 when, being fed up with the way in which her relatives treated her, she fled to the maquis taking with her a brother and two sisters all younger than herself. Armed with a rifle and pistol she presented herself at a woodcutter's camp and demanded work.

"You're only a child," they said. "You can't cut wood."

"Whatever a man can do I can do," she replied.

HER EXPLOITS

She got work and prospered sufficiently to buy a cottage, where she installed her brother and sisters. Though she interested herself in local politics until she dominated the whole neighborhood she remained a child of the maquis.

Many stories are told about Stellina's exploits, of which this is an example.

One day her pigs were stolen. For days she tramped the maquis until she found them on a farm. With gun in hand she ordered the owner of the farm to give up the stolen property, which he did. Then she drove the animals back to her own domain through 40 miles of thick scrub.

Today Stellina is an elderly dark-skinned Amazon with a black beard. She carries a rifle, cartridge bill, and two revolvers.

NAPOLEON'S FORCES

Corsican banditry dates back a hundred years, the first inhabitants of Corsica being bandits by profession – the Saracens.

In the third Napoleon's time bandits caused such trouble in the island that he was forced to send a force of old soldiers, known as the "Voligers Corses," to try and exterminate the outlaws. Many were killed and taken prisoners, but a few remained, and it is their descendants who are causing all the trouble today.

Previously a Corsican bandit was counted as an outlaw of honor. He took to the maquis after revenging insults against a member of his family.

Today the Corsican brigand tries to imitate the Chicago gangster, and in many cases he gets away with it. – Press Association Foreign Special.

"Corsican Outlaw Barely Gets Away. Chased From Lair to Lair Until His Nerves Become Shaky," *Chattanooga Daily Times* (Chattanooga, Tennessee), 28 February 1932, p. 13

Ajaccio. André Spada, the overlord of the Maquis, has just described for the information of a girlfriend how he spent his Christmas and New Year "holidays," hunted down from point to point, his Christmas dinner interrupted three times by the alarm of raiding police and soldiers. The letter has fallen into the hands of the police, and shows that Spada is feeling the pinch now.

"Christmas Eve," he says, "I passed in solitude in the place you know. I had collected from various sources the wherewithal for a modest meal, and had settled to it when my ears caught the sound of stealthy footsteps. I got up, pushing into my haversack the remains of my meal, and only got away in time. The gendarmes were on the trail, but how they learned of my hiding place is beyond me.

"I got safely to my other lair, and again settled down to my meal, but they must have trailed me, because I soon caught the ominous sounds again.

"So it was off again, but that night I woke up with the feeling that enemies were near, and in the darkness I seemed to see figures moving.

"They may have been real or fancy, but the main thing is that they did not find me in my hiding place.

"All the same, I thought it unwise to risk another day in this place, so made off once more, and my Christmas night I spent in a retreat known only to myself and one other man.

"But the feeling of insecurity and imminent peril was with me more than ever, and that my sense was not playing me tricks will be clear when I say that three times my supper was interrupted by the sound of suspicious movements. The first time I saw the pursuing gendarmes with the guide pass right under the ledge covering my hiding place.

"I was tempted to pay the guide for his treachery as only a Corsican can pay such baseness, but I reflected that it would only bring my enemies down on me, and my vengeance will keep.

"This first time they passed without seeing me or my den. The second time they disturbed me it seemed that they could not fail to discover my retreat.

"They were almost on me, my fingers touched the trigger and I was about to shoot when to my relief they turned away, baffled by the care with which I had concealed the 'door' of my hiding place.

"One other alarm that night. It came just as I was draining the last of my wine and settling down for the final smoke before rest, which I needed more than ever. The same party was approaching from the direction they had first come, cautiously and stealthily, with rifles ready to shoot at sight.

"They came nearer than ever this time, and again there came to me the sensation of the hunted animal for whom there is nothing but the fight to the death.

"Again I had the itch to release the trigger, but again my enemies failed to detect what they were looking for, or to see my eyes watching them through the cunningly arranged brush screen at my door.

"I went back to my couch, convinced that this was the last alarm of the night, and I was right."

The letter, written in the patois, has been identified as being in the handwriting of Spada, and the police are trying to find the woman to whom it was addressed in the hope that they may be able to wring from her the secret of his hiding place.

"'Herald' Talk with Hunted Bandit.
Spada Tells Why He will Never be Caught,"
Daily Herald (London), 7 March 1932, pp. 1, 3

From our Special Correspondent, Samuel Robinson, Île-Rousse (Corsica), Sunday.

André Spada, the uncrowned king of Corsica, is safe from arrest. He assured me of that last night when I met him within three miles of the village where the guards who are combing Corsica for him are quartered.

After securing the confidence of his relatives, and convincing them that I did not believe the stories of his death, or the rumors of his flight from Corsica, I persuaded them to arrange a secret meeting.

A closed car, with the blinds carefully drawn, came to my hotel. I was told to enter, and it was driven rapidly away in the dark.

We ran for some time up a very rough mountain path. Suddenly we stopped.

I was told to get out of the car, and I found that it was on a deserted footpath.

My guide led me to some brushwood, from which three heavily armed men appeared as if by magic.

They took me to a lonely shepherd's hut on the hillside, where I was introduced to Spada's right-hand man.

He questioned me, and I was searched for arms. Then he told me that I might see his chief.

Then came an hour's hard walking through fields, bushes, shrub and dwarf wood, to a lonely dwelling.

It was apparently miles from the nearest habitation or road, but, I learned afterwards, it was only three miles from a village.

I was bidden to enter, and there stood Spada himself, the man whose capture was sought by hundreds of soldiers and police.

"I will talk to the 'Daily Herald,'" he said, "but a police spy ..." He made a significant gesture and left the sentence unfinished.

He was a short, stockily built man, typically Corsican, and, although unshaven, unexpectedly clean. He seemed about 50 years old.

He asked me to drink with him some liquor named pastis, which tasted like absinthe.

We all drank together, and then the bandit asked me to sit down, and we talked.

"I have twenty men surrounding this building," he said, "and no one can leave or enter unless I wish it."

"How is your life now?" I asked, "since you are tracked day and night by hundreds of men."

He shrugged his shoulders. "As good as that of any man who is hounded by bloodhounds, but they will never take me alive."

"It is not the local authorities who worry me. It is the men from the mainland.

"They are not afraid of my vengeance.

"I am not to be classed with those men," he went on, "who have paid the penalty of their crimes recently, and whose names are a disgrace to Corsican banditry."

"I have been forced to live my life as I do through a vengeance of honor.

"During my term in the maquis, I have only extorted money. If they want to get me, a lot of blood will be spilled first."

Sparta rose and indicated that our conversation was at an end. I was to remain where I was for two hours to give the bandits time to get away. These days I have to take precautions, he remarked grimly as he went out.

I believe Spada – they will not get him alive.

"In Petticoats, Bandit Chief,"
The World's News (Sydney, Australia), 18 May 1932, p. 39

André Spada, Corsica's most notorious bandit, who eluded the police during their campaign to clean up the island last November, is being sought in the disguise of an elderly woman with pinched face and spectacles. According to reports, the police believe that Spada is living under the protection of an Englishwoman whom his romantic personality has inspired with admiration. Somewhere in the backwoods of Napoleon's Island it is thought that the former terror of Corsica – for Spada has long carried his life in his hands – is performing the duties of a housekeeper dressed in women's clothes and with a gray wig covering his black, bushy hair.

When investigations were made by gendarmes last November, a letter in English was found professing passionate attachment to the bandit and signed with a woman's name.

It is reported that the writer persuaded Spada to shave off his mustache, and, wearing women's clothes, to pass himself off as her middle-aged housekeeper, and in this disguise, it is suggested, the bandit passed unnoticed through the police lines to his present place of safety.

"English Woman and Bandit King. Visit to the Lair of André Spada," *Halifax Evening Courier* (Yorkshire, England), 9 March 1933, p. 2

Paris, Thursday.

André Spada, the notorious Corsican bandit, who has long been wanted by the French police, has emphatically denied the story that he once took refuge in the house of an Englishwoman who admired him. What he does admit is taking a meal with her when she came to his hiding place in the Corsican maquis.

The famous bandit, who has been interviewed in the maquis by Mme. Christine Hubert and Mr. Harry Grey, on behalf of "Paris-Soir," described how, one day just before the expedition which was to round up the bandits had arrived in the island, an old friend came to his hiding place, accompanied by the Englishwoman.

"I was furious," said Spada, "for it is an unwritten law that you must wait for a bandit of honor to come to you or send an invoice, but you must never seek him out. I treated the man as he deserved, but I asked the Englishwoman, because she was a woman, to take her meal with me and my friends. When she had rested a while, I provided her with a guide to take her back to Calcatoggio. That was the only time I saw her and everything else that has been said or written about her is false."

When the police searched Spada's house some time ago, they found a letter written by the Englishwoman in broken French and giving her version of the meeting with Spada. It is addressed to "His Majesty, the King of the Maquis" and began "Dear Mr. Spada." It thanks him "for the Royal Banquet at which I was, perhaps, too overcome to do it justice." – Reuter.

"Famous Outlaw Caught. Trapped in His Lair by Two Policemen. Jungle 'King,'" *Birmingham Gazette* (Birmingham, West Midlands, England), 30 May 30 1933, p. 13

Ajaccio, Corsica, Monday.

André Spada, "King of the Maquis," the most famous of Corsica's modern bandits, has been captured. He was trapped by two policemen as he was hiding in his lair near the town of Ajaccio.

It was less than eighteen months ago that the French government spent thousands of pounds and employed thousands of men in an attempt to wipe out banditry in Corsica and capture the leading bandits. Sparta eluded them.

Crime of Revenge

André Spada was the most famous of the outlaws who have ruled Corsica in recent years.

Known as "The Bandit of Honor" and "The King of the Maquis" (or "Jungle"), he led hundreds of French gendarmes in a merry chase when they swept through the island in the winter of 1931-32.

In 1925 he committed a crime which shocked Corsica. He forced Marie Caviglioli, sister of a famous bandit leader, to live with him. After months of quarreling she stabbed him and afterwards left him. In revenge he blinded her brother in one eye and cut out his tongue, and then killed the uncle and sister of Marie's new lover.

In 1930, having been deprived of a mail service concession, he attacked the car carrying the mail between a Ajaccio and Lopigna, killed the new concessionaire and two of the guards.

Englishwoman's Interview

Spada's friends pointed out that the bandit never killed to rob, but only to "avenge his honor," hence the name, "the bandit of honor." His capture was one of the principal tasks of the French expedition sent to the island.

The fame he acquired led hundreds of women to write love letters to him. An Englishwoman, Mrs. Edith Halford Nelson, who had interviewed him in connection with a series of articles she wrote for a Marseilles newspaper, was questioned by the French police for hours in an attempt to discover Spada's hiding place. Mrs. Nelson denied that she knew anything about the bandit apart from what she had learned when she interviewed him.

Spada made the boast last year that he would never be captured alive.

"Englishwoman Fights for Bandit," *Daily Herald* (London), 21 June 1933, p. 11

Nice, Tuesday. An Englishwoman arrived in France tonight to fight for the life of André Spada, the Corsican bandit king, who is to be tried at Bastia Assizes on a dozen charges of murder.

She is Mrs. Edith Halford Nelson, the novelist who befriended the bandit king when he was hunted by the French police.

She lived alone in an obscure corner of Corsica until, suspected by the police of being an accomplice of Spada, she found her life made intolerable for her.

Finally, she fled to sanctuary in the convent of Santo Vincenzo, in Florence.

When news of the bandit's arrest reached her a fortnight ago she returned at once to France, and tonight wrote to Spada at Ajaccio Prison, telling him to take heart.

She plans to brief Maitre de Moro-Giafferi, one of the foremost barristers in France, and himself a Corsican, to defend Spada at the Assizes.

She signed the letter, "Your admirer, Edith Halford Nelson."

"Story of Government's Plot To Kidnap Bandit King. Woman 'Smuggled Into Consulate,'" *Daily Herald* (London), 22 June 1933, p. 11

From Our Own Correspondent. Nice, Wednesday.

A startling story of a plot by the Italian government to kidnap André Spada, the Corsican bandit king, was told to me today by Mrs. Edith Halford Nelson, Spada's Englishwoman friend.

Spada, now held by the French authorities on charges of murder, is an Italian subject.

"Last September," Mrs. Nelson told me, "I was approached by the Italian government.

"I was asked to go to a hotel in Bastia (Corsica), where I found the Italian Consul waiting for me, and when it was dark I was smuggled into the Consulate.

FEARED A TRAP

"There, for more than an hour, I was alone with the Consul. He asked me to help him find André Spada, who was in hiding from the French police.

"He said, 'You know that Spada is an Italian, and we still hope that he is a good Italian. We want to get him out of Corsica and into Italy.'

"He went on to tell me that Spada possessed valuable knowledge about all the secret passes over the Corsican mountains which his government needed.

"Fearing a trap, however, I refused to say where my friend was.

"Finally the plot leaked out, and the Italian government warned me that it would be better for me to leave Corsica.

"I was told that the best thing for me to do would be to stay for a while in a convent in Florence."

Mrs. Nelson has now left the convent to make arrangements for the defense of Spada when his trial opens in November.[40]

---

[40] Upon reading this dispatch, Jules Mondoloni remarked: "The attempt to recover Spada, of Italian origin, by the consul in Bastia is in line with Mussolini's irredentist aims on the island, with the active complicity of the autonomist-regionalists of Corsica during the fascist era, who today have taken power in the Regional Assembly of Ajaccio."

"Dread of Guillotine. Corsican Bandit Goes on Hunger Strike," *Evening Despatch* (Birmingham, West Midlands, England), 11 April 1934, p. 3

Marseille, Wednesday.

André Spada, formerly one of the one of Corsica's most notorious bandits, went on hunger strike yesterday at the Chave prison in Marseilles, where he is under observation preparatory to his trial on charges of having committed twelve murders.

A warder had told Spada that the guillotine sent to Aix-en-Provence for the execution of Sarret[41] yesterday was coming back to Marseilles. Evidently Spada believed it was to be erected for him, for he at once refused to eat and for hours shrieked for mercy.

Actually the guillotine is on its way to Bastin for the execution of [Jean Baptiste] Torres, one of Spada's lieutenants.

Spada is being observed by alienists. His behavior for some months has been strange, and the authorities are inclined to the belief that the bandit is simulating insanity to escape the guillotine. – British United Press.

---

[41] Georges-Alexandré Sarret (1878 – 1934): a French criminal executed for committing a double murder, who was the last prisoner to be guillotined in Aix-en-Provence.

"Spada's Englishwoman Friend. 'He Has Never Had a Fair Chance.'" *Evening Post* (Nottingham, England), 8 March 1935, p. 6

Mrs. Edith Halford Nelson, the Englishwoman who has interested herself in Spada, the condemned Corsican bandit, when interviewed on the Riviera yesterday, wept hysterically over his death penalty.

"I am not surprised," she declared, "but, naturally, I feel terrible. Spada is not sane, and the guillotine was not a fair sentence. I would have done everything in my power to save him, as I told him, and I know he has never had a fair chance in his life.

"It is untrue that I was his lover. I only had a great admiration for his bravery, and was never afraid of him. He has a good heart."

Mrs. Nelson is at present writing articles about Corsican life.

Appendix B: Adventure in Corsica

**"Adventure in Corsica with the Bandit André Spada,"
by Edith Halford Nelson. From her memoir,
Out of the Silence (London: Rider and Co., 1944), pp. 76-80**

I had always longed to visit Corsica, and eventually found myself on this enchanted island. Here I met the famous bandit, André Spada, and if I mention here our strange friendship it is because it was brought about by my connection with Cheiro.

June in Corsica is the month when the bandit's title for the Maquis, '*Le Palais Vert*' (The Green Palace), best describes the perfumed wilderness of aromatic plants, thorny scrub and larch forests of which Napoleon writes in his memoirs – that if he were passing his island far out at sea he would know it by the scent, even if the island were invisible.

Of the modem Corsican bandits, André Spada was the only one who interested me sufficiently to make me want to have a closer acquaintance with him. His name, Spada – a sword – pleased me by its apt significance. I decided to write his life.

For months I tried various methods of approach, all of which ended in defeat. It was difficult to get people to speak freely concerning him, and one and all assured me of the futility, and also the danger, of my quest. They told me:

"No journalist has ever succeeded in getting near him. He does not seek publicity, and he is very suspicious of women, for they are often used as police spies. You will never get to see him; give it up."

All of which, naturally, made me the more determined to succeed.

I wrote that story, and it was published in serial form in one of the principal French newspapers, the *Petit Marseillais*. The story included my predictions concerning his fate.

This is how it came about:

I met a young man whose father owned a garage in Ajaccio. This young man, Jean Malandri, told me more about Spada than I had ever been able to obtain from other people. Then one day he turned his hawklike Corsican eyes on me and said quietly:

"Madame, it is no longer you who are looking for Spada, but he who is waiting to see you. My father and I have orders to bring you to him. Some of his men think you are a police spy; we have, I think, convinced him that you are not, but that is not his principal reason for sending for you. This reason, however, he has forbidden us to disclose to you."

I am writing of the time – 1931 – when Corsica, though only eight hours from Nice, was so entirely under bandit rule that the command of a bandit chief was law, and when not obeyed, the only other alternative, if you valued your life, was to take the next boat to the mainland, if you were lucky enough to be able to do so.

But I was too excited to think about the danger, and so I answered:

"How mysterious, how thrilling! When do we start?"

"Tomorrow at dawn. And remember, not a word to anyone – his life, yours, and ours depend on your silence."

"Of course."

Suddenly his rather fierce young face softened in a smile.

"And you will not be afraid to meet him?"

"Afraid? Of what? You have told me that be is both intelligent and pleasing, and I shall not be alone."

"No, you will not be alone, but what I meant was that André is really *un peu formidable* the first time one meets him. He is a walking arsenal of cartridge belts and revolvers, but he is a charming fellow – you will like him."

The place I was taken to was the famous 'Punte di Meurti' (Death's Point), the scene of Romanetti's orgies.

Perched on the highest pinnacle of the surrounding mountains was a long, low farm, hidden behind a natural fortress of gigantic rocks. Spada was converting it into a veritable armor plated, bullet-proof shelter when the expedition arrived which reduced his stronghold to ruins with machine guns and hand grenades. Spada escaped – by five minutes.

With my heart beating just a little faster at the thought, 'At last, after all, I *have* reached Spada, Sword of the Maquis,' I entered a small, bare, whitewashed room that opened directly on to the mountain side. As I did so a man rose from a table and came towards me holding out his hand in greeting. He was of medium height, dressed in dark-brown corduroy velvet and high boots. He wore two bandoliers stuffed with cartridges, into which were also thrust four revolvers, the leather holsters of which hung on the back of the chair from which he had just risen. Beside this chair a rifle rested against the wall. This 'veritable arsenal' that be was wearing made him look almost square.

His face, though rather heavy, was distinctly handsome. Brown hair turning grey at the temples waved back from an intelligent forehead, but it was the man's eyes which held one. Great yellow-brown eyes like those of a lion, and with the same fixed, unblinking alertness. For an instant they challenged my own, then he smiled and said:

"Madame, you are welcome. Come and sit down, you must be tired after that climb."

It was not until after an excellent lunch that Spada said to me, with the smile that, catlike, relieved his somewhat sinister face:

"Now, Madame, would you like to know why I have sent for you?"

"Because you thought that I was a police spy?" I enquired with a smile.

"No," he answered gravely; "though that might still have been in the back of my head, it isn't now; but remember never to speak of what you may see or hear when you are near me." His eyes narrowed; he put his hands on my shoulders, a gesture which caused me to stand up quite straight and meet the great eyes that suddenly flared into my own. Slowly, quietly and very distinctly Spada said:

"If – you – betray me, I will – *kill* – you."

I answered with a smile:

"Monsieur Spada, I have no intention of betraying you – *vous m'êtes très sympathique.*"

"André, why are you trying to frighten her?" asked Jean, who had come to my side, and Spada answered ironically:

"She is a woman; all women talk-too much; she had to learn her lesson." Then to me: "*Soit* – I believe you. Now let's talk of something pleasant." He turned away, calling for drinks to be brought.

"Sit down here beside me," he said to me in his gentle, purring voice, "and I will tell you why I have sent for you. Even here in the maquis we have heard of the great seer Cheiro. I am told that you can see into the future and that it was he who developed in you this gift. Tell me my future – tell me the truth."

"I will do my best," I answered, "but I am only an instrument controlled by vibrations in sympathy with, yet stronger than, my own. These conditions are not often found. First let me look into your right hand."

He placed his hand in mine and I remarked not so much on its strength – it looked as if he had only to close his fingers on my wrist to snap it like the stalk of a flower – but on the well-kept nails, which, however, were in keeping with the rest of the man. Spada was always clean-shaven and singularly well-groomed. The rough brown corduroy which he wore was impregnated with the scent of the maquis in which he lived.

I noticed two remarkable things in the lines of Spada's hand. The line of destiny was effaced, and by it another line ran, clear and incisive, as if carved with a knife. There was a star on the base of the little finger, which means captivity. I said to him:

"The destiny which should have been yours is effaced. You have carved out another for yourself. If people cross your will or stand in your path, you send them out of it."

A man's voice murmured:

"Sometimes as far as the next world."

I did not tell him about the star.

I asked him to hold my hands by the wrists, letting them rest lightly in his own, and to ask me what he wanted to know. To look into my eyes and to *will* the answers.

He took my hands as I had directed him, and his yellow eyes shot their unblinking, relentless gleam into my own.

"Tell me the truth," he commanded. "Tell me my destiny, what is going to happen to me in the near future?"

My eyes closed wearily; I sank back in my chair, and soon I heard my own voice speaking, distinctly, monotonously, like the voice of a sleepwalker; yet I was still conscious of my surroundings, though vaguely so.

"Soon you will be in some terrible danger."

"I am always in danger."

"This time it is much nearer, but you escape unhurt. Blood and brains spattered on what looks like a door – it is horrible, horrible!"

"When will this happen?"

"In three weeks' time."

I tried to draw my hands from his, but his fingers closed more firmly over my wrists and he said tensely:

"More – tell me more. What do you see?"

"A short time after you will be wounded very seriously in the head, and the neck, left side. It is the head wound that is serious, but you recover. The end is still far off – a town set at the foot of great hills – the sea – dawn – ah, no more, no more. I cannot, I *will* not see any more."

When I opened my eyes the room was full of men in velvet. Several, in order to get nearer to us, were lying full length across the table, and the others had crowded around, yet not touching our chairs. In the shadow of the doorway I caught the cold, hard gleam of a woman's eyes, set in a face that might have been Agrippina's.[42] This was Antoinette Leca, fitting chatelaine of Punte di Meurti. Spada got up and, walking to the door looking on to the terrace, stood looking out over the maquis.

"Make her drink something," he called over his shoulder. Jean Malandri gave me the water I asked for. I noticed that he was frowning heavily, and realized that in some way my predictions had created a danger cloud.

What was the strange force that had been at work? Probably the vibrations of an outlaw who neither knew nor asked for pity, who lived under the shadow of a violent death, in constant contact with Nature at her wildest and most primitive majesty. Probably also the vibrations of the place itself, which Spada told me is said to owe its name – Death's Point – to some great battle that was fought upon it way back in the mists and shadows of antiquity.

"There are many legends connected with this place," he said. "They say that spirits dance here when the moon is full. I have not seen them, but I know those that have." He spoke calmly as of a subject beyond dispute.

"Spirits dance here when the moon is full." His words seemed to knock at the door of remembrance. Astarte – the cult of the Moon. In Tunisia, on just such an inaccessible peak, my tent had been pitched beside the fallen columns and the sacrificial altar of a temple dedicated to the cult of the Moon Goddess.

Were the spirits that danced here on the Punte di Meurti those of the fair young men and maidens sacrificed to the pale goddess?

---

[42] A reference to the Roman empress Agrippina the Younger (15? AD – 59 AD), wife of Emperor Claudius and mother of Nero,

Three weeks later to a day, Spada killed the conductor of a postal service car and two gendarmes. A third was found unconscious in the car, which Spada had set on fire, but which fortunately had not continued to burn. I saw the car directly after the tragedy; *one of the doors was spattered with blood and brains.*

About a month later I was walking in the Greek village Carjess,[43] when the mayor of the village left the café where he was sitting and crossed the road to me. He said softly and intently:

"Madame, your friend has been wounded very seriously."

To which I answered immediately and quite calmly:

"Yes, I know, but he will recover."

The mayor frowned, fixing his dark eyes on my face, and he said ironically: "Excuse me, Madame, you say *you know*, but that is impossible. No one knows except myself and the doctor I have just taken to him." Something in my eyes must have intrigued him, for he said impatiently:

"Well, if you know – *where* has he been wounded?" .

"In the head and the neck, left side. It is the head wound that is dangerous, but he will get over it."

The mayor took a step back, his eyes widened.

"Madame!" he gasped. "But no, it is impossible, you cannot have seen him; it is too far off and it has only just happened. Madame, *je vous en prie, how* do you know ?"

I answered with a smile: "I cannot explain what I do not understand myself. I only know that I told him a month ago that this would happen to him. Ask him."

I moved away, leaving the mayor looking after me, silent and frowning, much as if he had seen a ghost.

I could fill a book with episodes of Spada as yet unwritten. The friendship of a hunted man must of necessity bring danger

---

[43] Possibly a variant spelling of Karyes, a village on the Peloponnese peninsula.

and complications; but I suffered chiefly from the annoyance, I may say jealousy, of certain journalists whom I had forestalled, and who, when I refused all interviews, first treated me as a charlatan and then, when my story was proved beyond doubt, gave to our friendship an entirely false, unpleasant, and very Latin atmosphere.

During the police expedition of 1931 – the real purpose of which was to fortify the island during a bad Italian scare – they filled their pockets with money with their stories, most of them lying ones, concerning the hunted bandit and his 'Amie Anglaise,' causing me in consequence great annoyance from the police; and when, two years later, May 30th, 1933, Spada was captured in his own village, worn out with privation and quite mad, they *one and all* turned against their hero, and accused him of feigning insanity to escape the guillotine, and prophesied that he would 'die like a dog.'

During the last weeks of his long imprisonment Spada regained his sanity. On the morning of his execution he was sleeping quietly when the governor of the prison entered his cell and awoke him.

"Spada," he said, "your hour has come – have courage."

And Spada answered quietly:

"I have never lacked courage. I shall not lack it now."   .

He walked unaided to the scaffold. As he reached it he turned his pale, haggard face towards where the dawn was just breaking over the sea, and the light shining in his yellow eyes showed them calm and resigned.

A moment later Spada – 'King of the Maquis' – died *like a King.*

ALSO BY ROB COUTEAU

Fiction:

Doctor Pluss
Afterword by Jim Feast

Essays and Interviews:

Collected Couteau

More Collected Couteau
Introduction by James Dempsey

*Portraits from the Revolution: Interviews with the
Protestors from Occupy Wall Street*

Biography:

*A Blind Man Crazy for Color. A Tribute to Leon Angély: Illustrated by
Picasso's Model and Muse, Sylvette David*

Poetry:

The Sleeping Mermaid
Introduction by Christopher Sawyer-Lauçanno

Selected Poems
Introduction by Ed Foster

Memoir:

Intimate Souvenirs
Introduction by Robert Roper

"Here we have a new, possibly classic memoir of New York. It begins in Gravesend, Brooklyn, and moves outward, to Manhattan and Paris ... That there still exists a path to a writer's life that is not a dutiful march through creative writing academies, with perhaps the apotheosis of becoming a teacher of yet more academy-shaped writers, is heartening to learn. Couteau does not make fun of that approach nor of any other, but he does model something much different, and to see him continuing to write books like this one, which well deserves a place on his already considerable shelf of valued books, is excellent news." – Robert Roper, author of *Nabokov in America: On the Road to Lolita* and *Now the Drum of War*.

"*Intimate Souvenirs* is a memoir with a message that embraces a coming-of-age story with a background in!1970s Brooklyn. This influenced Rob Couteau's progressive work as an adult with the homeless and impoverished, from America to Venezuela ... Couteau brings to vivid life his impressions of the world from an early age, and his evolving place in it ... As Couteau moves through different worlds (including France), encountering literary, artistic, and social figures, he finds a new sense of home, place, and purpose which translates to social and philosophical revelations about life, religion, and the world. Ultimately, his very method of engaging with other worlds is what links readers to his life and the exuberant march of its encounters and revelations.

Five hundred pages go by in the blink of an eye as readers absorb an intriguing memoir that deserves a place in any library strong in memoirs that embrace literary, artistic, and social transformation The book features an Introduction by acclaimed novelist Robert Roper and an Afterword by literary biographer Christopher Sawyer-Lauçanno." – Diane Donovan, Senior editor, *Midwest Book Review*.

A Blind Man Crazy for Color. A Tribute to Leon Angély: Illustrated by Picasso's Model and Muse, Sylvette David

"In the lanes and alleys of Paris, at the turn of the!9th century, a nearly sightless art collector wandered on the arm of a young girl. The collector, aided by his guide, amassed a treasure trove of work by the greatest artists of the day: Modigliani, Picasso, Utrillo, and more. Yet he died poor, forced to sell the work for a fraction of its value during the dark days of World War I. Little is known about the life – or the fate – of the girl who led the blind collector through the City of Light. This is the story of Léon Angély, the myopic lover of art, and Joséphine, the 'eyes' of Angély, the girl who enabled him to visit artists and 'see' their art. The story is told with a rare grace by author Rob Couteau in his new book, *A Blind Man Crazy for Color*. Couteau has mined the literature for gems, and displays them with abandon, through the generous quotations and anecdotes set within his own lustrous prose. The fine text is accompanied by enchanting illustrations by Sylvette David. In David, the book finds both painter and participant in the milieu Angély so loved: in!954, David began modeling for Picasso, becoming the 'girl with the ponytail' in hundreds of works, including the artist's monumental sculpture, *Sylvette*, in Rotterdam ... We found the friendship of Léon and Joséphine a balm for our souls, so bruised in these difficult days of violence and disease. We hope the story is healing for you, too."
– *Witty Partition*

"In his strange, fascinating new book, writer-painter Rob Couteau assembles and unearths what little can be known about the mysterious collector Léon Angély ... Adding another layer of resonance to Couteau's slim volume are the charming illustrations by Lydia Corbett, also known as Sylvette David, the ponytailed model and muse who inspired Picasso's 'Sylvette' period."
– Scott Sublett, *New Art Examiner*.

"Sylvette David's sketches accent this colorful portrait of Léon's life, motivations, involvement in the art world, and the pieces he collected. Previously unpublished information about the blind man's passion and his influence on the art world enhances a survey that should be required reading and acquisition for any serious art history student and the libraries catering to them ... Readers also receive revealing inspections of the process of interviewing artists and capturing their historical impact, adding to *A Blind Man Crazy for Color*'s importance as a survey that goes beyond a singular biography of an art enthusiast to delve into the world of artists, art appreciation, and muses ... Serious art libraries should consider this extraordinary recreation of artistic ambitions against all odds a mainstay that stands out in many different ways." – Diane Donovan, *Midwest Book Review*.

SELECTED POEMS

"There is a deep tenderness in these words, mingled with the sadness of age. If one goes back to the early poems addressed to Edda Maria Sangrígoli, one can find the tenderness there, too, as it is in his work as a case manager for the poor and homeless. There is much to admire in Couteau's oeuvre, but this tenderness stands out among so many things that make reading his work clearly an important experience."
– Ed Foster, founder of Talisman House Publishers, and editor
of *Talisman: A Journal of Contemporary Poetry and Poetics*.

"*Selected Poems* features 101 poems, 40 of which have been printed in numerous print and online journals since 1985. The rest are new to this collection and represent a satisfying blend of old and new works designed to appeal to newcomers and prior fans alike. Rob Couteau's works are diverse. They follow no set poetic structure, even defying some of them when the muse strikes and special needs indicate that the subject is more important than poetic form ... His inspections of artistic, literary, and social issues are astute and compelling. Don't anticipate set structures, uniform poetic approaches, or singular subjects. *Selected Poems* offers a freewheeling approach to poems and life alike and is a thought-provoking, evocative gathering of works recommended for literary readers not bound by convention or rules."
– Diane Donovan, *Midwest Book Review*.

"Couteau's essays are informal, fervent, and well-versed examinations of the work or author at hand. At their best, they include fascinating insights into the significance of a writer like Hubert Selby ... The interviews are uniformly strong and include conversations with Michael Korda on T. E. Lawrence, Justin Kaplan on Walt Whitman, and Robert Roper on Vladimir Nabokov. Not all of them focus on literature: author Jeffrey Jackson covers the 1910 flood of Paris and why it's relatively forgotten, and Robert De Sena, in one of the best interviews, discusses his life as a gang member turned community activist. Couteau's passion and wealth of knowledge are obvious throughout the book ... and should appeal to many readers."
– Publishers Weekly Select.

"The Renaissance Man is a multifaceted individual whose fingers are in just about every pie you could imagine, fostering a variety of abilities and mastering many quite well. His expertise is wide-ranging and there's seemingly no limit to his subject, as is demonstrated in More Collected Couteau: Essays and Interviews, which gathers Couteau's insights and encounters with a diverse range of individuals ...

The joy of reading Couteau's work lies as much in his penetrating, crystalline language as it does in the works or figures being examined, and so readers receive a wide-ranging treat that examines victims, vengeance, mortality, and immortality through an inspection process that educates even those unfamiliar with the subject: 'Selby once said: "There is no light in my stories, so the reader is forced to turn to his own inner light" to make it through this journey. I now realize this is only partially true. The great beacon in his demonic oeuvre is that of the artfully crafted line and the immense vision of wholeness and transcendence that lurks behind it. Selby's empathy is there, omnipresent, even while recording the darkest hues of black. The utmost depravity is portrayed with the noblest verse.'

After proving his prowess at the essay form, he turns to the heart of the collection: its interviews ... One of the pleasures in this collection is that readers needn't have prior familiarity with the writers' works. Couteau provides that familiarity by the structure of his interview questions, which probe the foundation beliefs of each figure ... From the possibility that Nabokov suffered unconscious doubts about his own value that led him to insist that the world acknowledge him as a genius to the underlying patriotism of counterculture icons who were commonly seen as rebels ('Ginsberg continually affirmed that, essentially, Jack had always been a sort of patriotic American,' says Sawyer-Lauçanno. 'This had never not been part of who he was. It was patriotic to get into an automobile made in Detroit and drive across the country'), both essays and interviews are designed to make readers think about underlying psychology, social perceptions, and cultural change.

Readers seeking not just a literary presentation but a lively analysis of selected wordsmiths and their lives and influences must add *More Collected Couteau* to their reading lists. It's a powerful presentation that offers much insight ... and which should find its way into many a college classroom as well." – Diane Donovan, *Midwest Book Review*.

"Good luck trying to pin down Rob Couteau. Name the genre, and Couteau has almost certainly been there and done that. Poet, novelist, essayist, critic, journalist, memoirist, and travel writer, Couteau is not one to be hampered by constraints. He passes easily from one form of literature to another as if the borders between them did not exist for him. Perhaps they don't.

Couteau has been called a 'literary enthusiast,' and although he certainly is enthusiastic about literature (and indeed all art), the phrase carries the smack of the amateur about it, and Couteau is anything but. He is, in fact, an undeniably consummate professional. He is an independent scholar in every meaning of the word – unaligned with any institution except for the literary and artistic canon he so loves, and a thinker who comes to his own conclusions ...

This collection gives the reader a good sampling of Couteau's literary and scholarly talents, not the least of which are his interviews with writers he admires. Having spent many years as a journalist, I believe I have some ability to recognize and admire an artful interviewer, and Couteau is a master. His preparation is comprehensive, meticulous, and profound. His understanding of the process of writing in so many genres allows him insights into the particular problems faced by the writers he interviews. His style is conversational and relaxed, but deceptively so; he is always in control of the interview. This said, however, when a sudden fact or insight takes the interview down unexpected pathways, Couteau has the aesthetic nimbleness to recognize the opening and to follow it.

The collection features interviews with biographers, memoirists, historians, an inner-city antiviolence activist, and the creator of LSD. You'll also find herein Couteau's writings on literature, which I hesitate to call criticism since they lack the worst features of much literary criticism, which can be clogged with so much pretentiousness, cant, and philosophical obfuscation that it would take a plunger of Brobdingnagian proportions to restore a healthy flow. Couteau's essays are often rhapsodic appreciations and evocations of the work under study, and are stuffed with both insights and joy.
– James Dempsey, author of *The Tortured Life of Scofield Thayer*.

THE SLEEPING MERMAID

"Novelist and literary enthusiast Rob Couteau brings readers part of his love with *The Sleeping Mermaid*, a book of flowing poetry and thought that asks plenty of questions and offers plenty of answers. *The Sleeping Mermaid* is a poetry collection well-worth considering."
– Willis M. Buhle, *Midwest Book Review*.

"In Couteau's work there is no phoniness, no artifice for the sake of artifice – though in the great French tradition this poet knows so well, there is some art for the sake of art. Couteau does not venture into realms of obscurity where meaning is confined to the interior of a Klein bottle; his poems all have direct force, subjects, even verbs. He is intent on having his readers share in his observations, whether it be his artful retelling and reinterpretations of Native American story and song, or his appraisal of how a woman parades across the avenue. He does not ever sacrifice ordinary sense for an extra-ordinary significance. Instead, he speaks with fervor, with something to say, with something he wants us to hang onto and, in the process, come to an understanding of why it matters not just to him but should matter to us.

I think it was William Carlos Williams who said that poetry is belief. Couteau believes in belief, believes that poetic worth is measured in faithfulness to what is, what has been, and what could be. These are his talismans; these are the points where he begins and ends. His poetic excursions take us to many places: to the Paris of Rimbaud and Picasso, to the Native North Americans, to mythology and history and how the woman he is encountering is seducing him as he seduces her (and us), and finally, how alone, the cosmos plays itself out at 3 a.m. when the only lap dog is memory."
– Christopher Sawyer-Lauçanno.

PORTRAITS FROM THE REVOLUTION: INTERVIEWS WITH THE PROTESTORS FROM OCCUPY WALL STREET

"Most American readers will harbor a prior, casual familiarity with the Occupy Wall Street movement of 2011 based on newspaper headlines and events of the times; but for a more in-depth survey of the philosophies, approaches, and concerns of the protests, *Portraits from the* Revolution is the item of choice, offering unprecedented depth and detail on the history and lasting impact of the Occupy Wall Street movement.

Chapters explore not just each individual's actions but their backgrounds, reasons for participating in Occupy Wall Street, and their experiences. And it offers criticism of media reporting of the movement's history, intentions, and approaches.

From how participants decided to react to violent antagonism against the Occupy movement to the social and political ramifications of not just Occupy but the elements it opposed, these interviews capture participants from all walks of life, from teens to full-time workers, and turn the newspaper reports into a series of personal vignettes about Occupy's deeper meaning.
– Diane Donovan, *Midwest Book Review*

DOCTOR PLUSS, WITH AN AFTERWARD BY JIM FEAST

"Intellectual freshness, richness, and potency ... Couteau is an impressively creative writer, whom Barney Rosset urged me to review." – Jim Feast, *Evergreen Review*.

"Rob Couteau describes *Doctor Pluss* as 'fiction based on actual dialogues with schizophrenic patients, diabolically "sane" psychotherapists, and well-meaning yet unerringly destructive social workers. It chronicles the descent of an eccentric, sardonic, and witty psychiatrist into what appears to be a state of complete madness.'

His intention to metaphorically and realistically portray and contrast the madness of psychiatric process as well as its patients is powerfully wrought in a story about patients 'surviving this holocaust of forgetfulness.' During this process, their identities and personalities are lost in the institutional morass of a center purported to excel in rehabilitation, but which actually contains many ethical and personal challenges to the new psychiatric resident at the Walt Whitman Asylum for Adults, Dr. Pluss.

It's a place of rage and despair, of ambiguity where hope and horror run close together, and daily gives Dr. Pluss pause for thought about his patients and his role in their lives: 'In her own unwitting way,' Pluss mused, Evelyn personified the dual aspects of the godhead: horror and joy; awe and fascination.'

Novellas typically are hard-hitting but often artificially succinct in their brevity. Often, one is left wanting for more. The best of them (of which *Doctor Pluss* is one) excels in taking this succinctness to its most logical conclusion, creating slices of life which are narrow enough to receive full-bodied flavor as the plot and characters develop.

One does not wish for more in *Doctor Pluss*. It's complete unto itself, exceptionally well developed, and emotionally compelling, connecting metaphorical traditional roles of doctor and patient, linking them in unexpected ways.

Couteau is not afraid to push the literary boundaries of convention in pursuit of a different form of descriptive truth, bringing readers along in a rollicking ride through schizophrenic experience that ultimately questions the foundations of reality and perception from both sides of the therapist's couch. His interpretations and descriptions of the schizophrenic experience are particularly astute, astonishing, and evocatively described ...

Readers who choose *Doctor Pluss* are in for a treat. It's like *One Flew Over the Cuckoo's Nest* on steroids: a thought-provoking examination of sanity, insanity, and the crossover process that leaves readers thinking long after this therapeutic slice of life is consumed.

– Diane Donovan, *Midwest Book Review*

www.ingramcontent.com/pod-product-compliance
Lightning Source LLC
Chambersburg PA
CBHW071717120626
46550CB00001B/267